Growing Out: From Disciples to Disciplers

GROWING IN LEADERSHIP

Carl Simmons

Group
Loveland, Colorado
group.com

Group resources actually work!

This Group resource incorporates our R.E.A.L. approach to ministry. It reinforces a growing friendship with Jesus, encourages long-term learning, and results in life transformation, because it's

Relational
Learner-to-learner interaction enhances learning and builds Christian friendships.

Experiential
What learners experience through discussion and action sticks with them up to 9 times longer than what they simply hear or read.

Applicable
The aim of Christian education is to equip learners to be both hearers and doers of God's Word.

Learner-based
Learners understand and retain more when the learning process takes into consideration how they learn best.

SEASON FIVE

Growing Out: From Disciples to Disciplers

GROWING IN LEADERSHIP

Visit our website: **group.com**

Credits

Editor: Lee Sparks
Editorial Director: Rebecca L. Manni
Chief Creative Officer: Joani Schultz
Assistant Editor: Alison Imbriaco
Art Director: Paul Povolni

Book Designer: Jean Bruns
Cover Designer: Holly Voget
Illustrator: Wes Comer
Print Production: Paragon Prepress
Production Manager: Peggy Naylor

Unless otherwise indicated, all Scripture quotations are taken from the *Holy Bible,* New Living Translation, copyright © 1996, 2004. Used by permission of Tyndale House Publishers, Inc., Carol Stream, Illinois 60188. All rights reserved.

ISBN 978-0-7644-4006-9

10 9 8 7 6 5 4 3 2 1   19 18 17 16 15 14 13 12 11 10

Printed in the United States of America.

Contents

What Growing Out Looks Like

Growing Out is more than a series of Bible studies—it's a progression that will take you and your group from becoming disciples of Jesus to becoming disciplers of *others* in Jesus. As you move through each season, you'll grow from the inside out—and as you grow, your life in Jesus will naturally expand and branch out to others in your world.

And here's the best part: As you grow out together, you'll realize how much you're *already* discipling others—starting with those in your group!

Growing Out is designed to allow you to jump in at the most appropriate place for you and your group. To help you discover your entry point, take a look at these descriptions of each season:

Season One: Growing in Jesus focuses on developing your relationship with Jesus. Because, let's face it, the first person you have to disciple is *yourself.* More to the point, you need to learn how to let Jesus *show* you how to be his disciple. So in this season, we focus on your relationship with Jesus and how to deepen it through spiritual disciplines such as prayer, worship, Bible study…and, not least of all, through your relationships with other Christians (such as the ones you're sitting with).

After you've been grounded in your relationship with Jesus, how does that shine into the rest of your life? That's where *Season Two: Growing in Character* comes in. This season focuses on how you can invite Jesus into your most important relationships—with your family, your friends, and the people you work with—and how to keep Jesus at the center of all of them.

Season Three: Growing in Your Gifts focuses on discovering the gifts, talents, and passions God has given you and how God might want to use them to serve others—whether that's inside or outside your church walls. After this season, you'll have a better sense of who God has created you to be, and why.

And with that, you're ready for *Season Four: Growing Others.* If you've gotten this far, you've developed and deepened your walk with Jesus, you've learned how to actually live it out among those people you most care about, and you've begun to discover how God has uniquely built you. Now…how do you take what God has shown you and help *others* walk through the same process?

If you've completed Seasons One through Three, you already know the answer because that's *exactly* what you've been doing with your group. Season Four will help you reach out to even more people. Call it mentoring, discipling, or just being a good Christian friend to someone who needs it. After Season Four, you'll be ready to come alongside anyone who's ready to have a deeper relationship with Jesus. Just as you were in Season One.

In the final two seasons, you'll explore what it takes to lead others where God wants you *and* them to go next. Because as you've walked through the first four seasons, guess what? You've been growing. Others know it. And God is honoring it. So whether you see yourself that way or not, God has matured you to the point where you're ready to lead. And we're going to help you get *more* ready.

Season Five: Growing in Leadership focuses on how to stay functional even as you learn how to lead. You'll walk together through the challenges of leadership—communication, conflict resolution, building consensus, learning how to adjust your ministry, and learning to stay focused on God instead of "*your* ministry."

And as you keep growing out, God may well put things on your heart that you'll need to be the one to initiate. That brings us, at last, to *Season Six: Growing in Your Mission.* God has given you a specific vision for ministry, and now you literally need to make the dream real. We'll help walk you through the issues that come with a God-given vision. Issues like, first of all, how do you know it really *is* God and not just you? How do you get others on board (and praying—a *lot*)? And how will *you* keep growing, even as the vision continues to grow and take shape?

Because, no matter where you are, you never stop *growing out*. God will always see to that.

Enjoy Growing Out, and may God bless you as you grow out together!

Why R.E.A.L. Discipleship Works

Before we go any further, take one more look at the copyright page of this book (it's page 2—the one with all the credits). Go to the top of the page where it declares, "Group resources actually work!" Take a minute or two to read that entire section describing Group's R.E.A.L. guarantee, and then come back to this introduction. I'll wait for you here…

Now that we're literally back on the same page, let's explore R.E.A.L. a little more deeply. Your desire to go deeper is the reason you're reading this book, and it's not only our goal but also our *passion* to help you accomplish that desire. When it comes right down to it, there's nothing more R.E.A.L. than discipleship. Think about it:

Relational

At the heart of it, discipleship *is* relationship. First and foremost, it's about developing the most important relationship you'll ever have— your relationship with Jesus. And as your relationship with Jesus grows, it becomes far more than anything you've ever imagined.

Like any great relationship, it doesn't develop on its own. It's intentional. It's work. But it's way more than that. What we get back is far more than what we put in. How could it *not* be? It's a relationship with *Jesus*. And as that relationship grows, we'll want to bring Jesus into every other relationship we have.

So we've kept that in mind as we've designed these sessions. You'll gain a deeper understanding of God's Word, but even more important, you'll discover how to share what you've learned with those around you. And that discovery *has* to happen in community. We've made these sessions very relational because, after all, you're learning how to become discipl*ers*. By definition, that means learning how to speak God into others' lives. As you do that, you'll get as much back as you give, if not more. Because that's what happens in great relationships.

You'll notice that we often suggest getting into pairs or smaller groups. That's because participation—and learning, not to mention life change—increases when everyone's involved. It's more challenging, sure, but it's also more rewarding. Be sure to take advantage of the times we suggest it.

All this is a long way of saying that by the time you've finished this season, you'll not only have a deeper relationship with Jesus, but your spiritual relationships with others will be richer and deeper than you had ever anticipated. And when that happens, be sure to thank us; a little affirmation goes a long way toward helping us to keep doing what we do here.

Experiential

Experiences? Yeah, we've got experiences. And as you discover together where God wants to take you next, you'll have experiences of your own long after you've completed these sessions.

Research has proven again and again that the more senses we engage in the learning process, the more likely a session is to stick and truly become woven into our daily lives. Jesus knew that, too. That's why he used everyday items to make his message more real. Not only that, but he invited people out of their comfort zones to conquer their fear of the unknown. We like to do that, too. A lot.

And because it's so different from what we're used to when studying God's Word, this is often the hardest part of R.E.A.L. learning for people to embrace. Is it *really* OK to have fun when we're studying the Bible? Does it truly honor God? Wouldn't it distract us from focusing on God?

First, let's make it clear that these are legitimate concerns. I've wrestled with all of them as I've developed these sessions. We want to honor Jesus. Discipleship isn't a joke. It's serious business. It's about the rest of your life and how you'll glorify God with it. There's nothing more serious than that.

Nonetheless, sometimes the best way to get serious is to set aside our expectations, so we're able to open up and get down to what we're *really* wrestling with, rather than just come up with the right answers, go home, and never really deal with the things God wants us to deal with. The experiences in this book go a long way toward accomplishing that. Here are just a few of the ways people "got R.E.A.L." as we field-tested this curriculum:

- A church elder in our group declared from the beginning, in no uncertain terms and with a bit of a growl, "I don't *do* games." A few weeks in, he shared, "This is exactly what [my wife and I] needed right now." Several weeks later, this same game-hating elder proclaimed, "I really *liked* that activity! It worked *perfectly*!"

- One of our hosts, who also prepared the session's snack, suggested, "I'll make sure I pull it out of the oven just when everyone gets here." She understood that not only the look and taste of the snack but also the smell would help people experience the session more acutely.

- A pastor in our group enjoyed one particular activity so much that he went ahead and used it in his own church's small-group training class.

- Another woman shared how her husband had been initially skeptical about R.E.A.L. learning and about small groups in general. (Anyone else detecting a pattern among the men, by the way?) Several sessions later, she was positively glowing as she shared how we'd "broken through" and how much he'd opened up as we'd gone along—and for that matter, how he was still talking about the session the next morning.

Discipleship *is* a lifelong adventure. And we're here to help you embrace that adventure. Together. That's why we've not only built in activities to get you thinking about your faith (and expressing it) in brand-new ways, but...well, let's just move on to...

Applicable

This is pretty straightforward. You're here not only to learn, but also to grow. And that means taking what you've learned and using it.

We give you opportunities in every session to do that—to give you a safe place to experiment, if you will. We also provide opportunities at the end of each session for you to take what you've learned and "Walk It Out!" in the rest of your life—so that your faith *becomes* your life, and you can take practical steps toward sharing your life in Jesus so others can see and respond to it as well.

Learner-Based

For some of you, the Bible passages and ideas you're studying may be familiar. But as you explore them in fresh ways in these sessions, you'll experience and understand God's Word in ways you've never considered before. We're studying God's living Word, after all. So we want to help you not only learn brand-new things, but also find new significance and meaning in familiar and taken-for-granted ideas.

Therefore, we've been very deliberate about choosing the right approaches for the right sessions. When an activity works, let's get up and do it. If a movie clip brings out the meaning of what you're learning, throw in the DVD and let's talk. If a snack not only works as an icebreaker but also as a discussion starter about a much deeper subject, let's serve it up and dig in. And when it's time to just open up God's Word and really wrap our minds around what God wants us to understand about a given subject—or to be reminded of what God has already shown us (because we forget that all too easily, too)—then we'll bust out our Bibles and read as many passages as it takes to begin to grasp (or re-grasp) that.

You're also here to discover who *you* are in Jesus. The body of Christ is made of millions of unique parts. You're one of them. We *know* one size doesn't fit all, and we've built Growing Out to reflect that. So whatever reaches you best—the Bible study, the activities, the questions, the take-home pieces, whatever—use them to their fullest extent. I'll give you some more ideas of how to do this in the next two sections.

However you approach these sessions—and whether you do that as a leader or as a participant—be sure to help others in your group approach things in the ways God can best reach them. And as God works in all of you, celebrate it. A lot.

May God bless you as you begin your journey together. And as God takes each of you to the places and experiences he has prepared for you, never forget: You're all in this together. You, God, and everyone he puts in your path. And *that's* discipleship.

—*Carl Simmons*

About the Sessions

Now that you know why we do what we do, let's talk about *how* we do it—and more important—how *you* can do it.

You may already understand this, but just so we're clear: Discipleship is *not* about completing a curriculum. It's about developing and deepening the most important spiritual relationships you have—first with God and then with those God brings you in contact with—because *none* of those relationships is an accident. They're all intentional, and we need to be intentional as well.

In fact, that's why we refer to each study as a season, rather than as a study, book, or quarter. We grow individually, at our own pace. Your season of growth might be longer or shorter than someone else's, and that's OK. God will take as long as you need to get you where he wants you. So spend as much time in each season as you need to. But stay committed to moving forward.

Also, each season has been built so that whether you're a participant or a leader, you can get the most out of each session. And that starts with the layout of each lesson. Keep a finger here, flip over to one of the sessions, and let's look at why this is so different.

This isn't just a leader guide. It's not just a guide for group members. It's *both*! And the way we've set up the sessions reflects that.

Leaders: The left-hand pages contain *your* instructions, so you're constantly on track and know what's happening next. What you do, what you say—all the basics are there. You'll also want to be sure to check out "Leader Notes" beginning on page 153. They'll give you specific prep instructions for each session, as well as great tips to make each session the best it can be.

Group Members: You don't care about all that leader stuff, do you? Didn't think so. Now you don't need to. The right-hand pages are just for you. Write your answers, journal whatever else God is saying to you, record insights from your group discussions, doodle while you listen—you've got plenty of room for all of it. All the questions and Bible passages you'll be using are right there. Use your pages to get the most out of what God's showing you each week.

Got all that? Good. Now let's talk about what each session looks like.

Come and See
In this (usually) brief opening section, you'll take time to unwind and transition from wherever you're coming from—a hectic drive to church on a Sunday morning or the end of a busy day—into the theme of the session. You and your group might enjoy a snack or a movie clip together; maybe it'll be an activity; maybe you'll just talk with someone else. Then you'll be ready to dig in deep. And maybe—because you were too busy having such a good time doing it—you won't even realize that you've already gotten down to business.

Seek and Find
This is the heart of each session and usually the longest section. You'll spend roughly a half-hour digging into God's Word and discovering its meaning in a way you hadn't realized before. You think you understand these things now? Just *wait*. Through a variety of experiences and powerful questions that take a fresh look both at Scripture and at what's going on in your own head and heart, you'll discover how God's Word *really* applies to your life.

Go
You'll move from understanding how what you've been studying applies to your life to considering ways to act on it. Through meaningful experiences and questions, you'll discover what you can do with what God has shown you through today's session. Which will take you directly into…

Walk It Out
This is the take-home part of the session. Past seasons of Growing Out provided specific suggestions for applying the session's lesson in practical ways. If you've gotten this far, however, you don't *need* suggestions. You just need to figure out how what you're learning applies to what you're already doing. And the only person who can answer that is you.

So in Seasons Five and Six, Walk It Out is an open-ended proposition. With a partner or partners, choose a weekly challenge that applies to what God's telling you about your situation. And then be obedient. Share what God is showing you with your group so they can pray for you and encourage you.

Go Deeper

I can't emphasize this enough, so I'm repeating it: Discipleship is *not* about completing a curriculum. It's about developing and deepening the most important spiritual relationships you have—first with God and then with those God has brought you in contact with—because *none* of those relationships is an accident.

Therefore, it's possible you'll work through this season and think, Before I go any further, I really need a deeper understanding of... That's why I've provided a list of resources at the end of each session to help you do just that. At Group, we're not shy about recommending other publishers—and if a resource applies to more than one area of spiritual growth, we'll recommend it more than once. This isn't about selling Group products (although there's always much more dancing in the halls here when that happens). It's about your growing relationship with Jesus and being willing to invite God into whatever you're still wrestling with.

And that painful thing you're feeling when you do that? That's called growth. But the good news is, we're in this together. So pull over whenever you need to! Or jump right into the next season. We're here for you either way.

Which brings us to a little reminder at the very end of each session: If there's an area in which you'd like to see *us* dig deeper and create more resources to help *you*, tell us! Write to us at Group Publishing, Inc., P.O. Box 481, Loveland, CO 80539; or contact us via e-mail at smallgroupministry.com. We'd love to hear what you're thinking. (Yes—*really!*)

Choose Your Environment

Growing Out works well in a variety of venues. We want to help you wherever you are. Don't be shy about trying any of them! Here are some additional ideas, depending on your venue.

Sunday School

First, you may have noticed that I've chosen the word *group* instead of *class* throughout. Not every group is a class, but every class is a group. You're not here just to study and learn facts—you're also here to learn how to live out what you've learned. Together. As a group. We hope that becomes even truer as you work through these sessions.

We've constructed these sessions to run an hour at a brisk pace, but we understand the limitations a Sunday school program can put on the amount of time you spend on a session. So if a great question has started a great discussion and you don't want to cut it off, feel free to trim back elsewhere as needed. For example, since many of the people in our field-test group were couples who could talk on the way home, we discovered that making Walk It Out a take-home instead of an in-class piece was one good way to buy back time without losing impact.

Try not to be one of those groups that say, "Great—we can skip that experience now!" Remember, the more senses and learning styles you engage, the more these sessions will stick. So play with these activities. Give yourself permission to fail—but go in expecting God to do the unexpected.

And if you don't have specific time limitations, read on.

Small Groups

If you need more than an hour for a session—and you're not tied to a clock or a calendar—take it! Again, taking the time to understand what God wants to tell your group is *way* more important than "covering the material" or staying within the one-hour or 13-week parameters. This happened repeatedly while field-testing—a great discussion ensued, people got down to things they were really wrestling with, and we decided we'd explore the session further the following week.

Learn to recognize rabbit trails—and get off of them sooner rather than later—but don't short-circuit those occasions when the Holy Spirit is really working in people's lives. Those occasions will happen often in these sessions. If you're having a rich discussion and are really digging in, take an extra week and dig even deeper. Give the full meaning of the session time to sink in.

One-on-One Discipleship

Although this curriculum is designed for a larger group setting, we absolutely don't want to discourage you from using it in a more traditional, one-on-one discipleship setting. True, some of the activities might not work in a setting this small, and if that's the case, feel free to bypass them and go directly into the Bible passages and questions—there are plenty left to work with. The important thing is that you work together through the issues themselves, at the pace that let's you move forward.

But don't take this as an opportunity to entirely excuse yourselves from experiences—have a little fun together, and see what God does. Allow yourselves to be surprised.

Also—and it's probably obvious for this and the next scenario—all those recommendations we make to form smaller groups or twosomes? You can skip those and jump right into the discussion or activity.

Smaller Groups or Accountability Groups

One more thing: We don't want to discourage you from doing one-on-one discipleship, especially if you've already got a good thing going. There are some great and healthy mentoring relationships out there, and if you're already involved in one, keep at it! That said, research has shown repeatedly that learning can happen at a more accelerated rate—and more profoundly—in settings other than the traditional teacher-student relationship. So if you're just starting out, consider gathering in groups of three or four.

- It's an environment that allows everyone to learn from others in the group. While there's often still a clear leader, the playing field feels more level, and the conversations often become more open and honest.

- If one person leaves for any reason—and there are plenty of legitimate ones—the group or accountability relationship isn't finished. Everyone else presses forward. No one is left hanging.

- The dynamics of a group of three or four are simpler than those of larger groups. And a group of three or four can be the best of both worlds, offering the rich discussions of a large group and the intimacy and accountability of one-on-one relationships.

- Again, we're about creating disciplers, and a smaller group allows growing disciplers to test-drive their own instructions, struggles, and transparency in an environment in which they can be both honestly critiqued and wholeheartedly encouraged. And when that happens, growth happens—for everyone.

If you'd like to delve into this subject further, Greg Ogden's *Transforming Discipleship* (InterVarsity) is a great resource to get you started, as are any number of materials from ChurchSmart Resources (churchsmart.com).

Whatever setting or environment you use for Growing Out, use it to its fullest. May God bless your efforts and those of the people with whom you share life!

Getting Connected

Pass your books around the room, and have people write their names, phone numbers, e-mail addresses, and birthdays in the spaces provided. Then make it a point to stay in touch during the week.

name	phone	e-mail	birthday

Leadership: *God's Definition*

"Obey your spiritual leaders, and do what they say. Their work is to watch over your souls, and they are accountable to God. Give them reason to do this with joy and not with sorrow" (HEBREWS 13:17).

In this session, we'll journey...

from ⟶ **to**
understanding God's view of leadership...

learning how to honor God's call to leadership—ours and others'.

Before gathering, make sure you have...

○ blackboard or white board✳

○ equal number of pennies, nickels, dimes, and quarters—enough so there's one coin for each person✳

○ small bowl for each group of four✳

✳See **Leader Notes**, page 155, for details.

Come and See

(about 15 minutes)

》 Welcome. Let's jump right in to today's session. Get into groups of four.

Give everyone time to group up.

》 We'll be exploring how to become the kinds of leaders God wants us to be—wherever God has placed us, whatever the situation. But before we dig in, let's take a few minutes to look at what God has done in our lives already to prepare us for *this* season of growth.

In your groups, take a minute each to introduce yourselves. Share briefly but specifically

• how God has grown you to the point where you're ready for a study on leadership; and

• what you hope God will accomplish in your life this season.

When you're done with introductions, discuss these two questions in your groups. We'll come back together in 10 minutes. ———

> *Not every Christian is called to major leadership in the church, but every Christian is a leader, for we all influence others. All of us should strive to improve our leadership potential.*
>
> —J. Oswald Sanders, *Spiritual Leadership*

After 10 minutes, come back together as a larger group. Share highlights and insights from the discussion time. Write responses to the question, What makes someone a *spiritual* leader? on your blackboard or white board.

》 You're all leaders, whether you have a spiritual gift of leadership or because God has blessed you by putting you where others rely on you. No matter how you got

here, you're leading in some way even now, and God wants to help you lead better.

And the better leadership God wants to lead you to isn't just in church—it's in your family, at work, even among your friends. You're here today because God has grown and matured you, and whether you see yourself as a leader or not, *someone* does. So let's honor the faith that others have placed in us. And while we're at it, let's better understand how we can honor those God has already raised up as *our* leaders.

▼ **GROUP**

◎ What makes someone a *spiritual* leader?

◎ Who have you seen demonstrate that kind of leadership? How?

Seek and Find

(about 25 minutes)

》 **Let's look at a couple of different examples of leadership from God's Word. May I have a couple of volunteers read Luke 7:1-11 and Acts 6:1-7?** ————

Have people get back into their groups. Get ready to pass your bowls of coins around.

》 **Whoever selects the coin with the highest value will be your group's leader for this next part of the session.**

Leaders: Have volunteers read 1 Peter 2:4-9 and 13-20, and then guide your groups through these questions.

Let's plan to come back together in 10 minutes. ————

Regain everyone's attention after 10 minutes, and ask people to stay with their groups. Share highlights and insights from the discussion time, and then discuss the following questions together. ————

Luke 7:1-11; Acts 6:1-7

◎ What different types of leadership can you find in these passages?

◎ How do you see authority being both recognized and honored by others in these passages? What happens as a result?

 1 Peter 2:4-9, 13-20

◎ What connections do you see in this passage between trusting God's authority and trusting human authority? How might *all* authority be seen as spiritual?

◎ Does rejecting human authority mean rejecting Jesus? Why or why not?

◎ So how did each of you feel after seeing the coin you selected? Disappointed? Relieved? Something else? Explain.

◎ How were your reactions like your usual reaction when the opportunity to lead arises? How much worth do you attach to being a leader?

◎ When have you been able to take the lead with something that really mattered to you? What did you learn from the experience?

Go

(about 20 minutes)

Read Hebrews 13:7-8 and 17-19, and then discuss these questions:

》 A little while ago, you shared about examples of leadership you've seen in your own lives. Starting today, you'll have some new examples to observe—in the group you're sitting with right now. You'll be working with these people for the rest of this season and exploring these ideas together. You're going to lead each other. You're going to learn from each other. And you're going to let God lead *you,* together. Be prepared for God to surprise you this season, and enjoy the surprises.

Right now you'll work in your groups to help each other walk out what God has been showing you today. Let someone who hasn't led yet lead this piece. Let's come back together in about 10 minutes.

Walk It Out (about 10 minutes)

How does what you learned today apply to where you're at right now? How can you put it into practice? Take 10 minutes in your groups to write one thing you'll do this week to make today's lesson more real in your own life. Share your choices with your group, and make plans to connect before the next session to check in and encourage one another.

✝ Hebrews 13:7-8, 17-19

◎ How does knowing that your leaders "watch over your souls, and they are accountable to God" (verse 17) affect the way you see them?

◎ Without naming names, describe a spiritual leader you know who *truly* loves God but with whom you nonetheless have trouble working? How *can* you see God working in him or her, and how can you honor that more openly?

◎ This time we'll name names: How do you still struggle with seeing *yourself* as a spiritual leader? What would you want God to change about yourself right now?

Because God gives authority to those who honor it, I'll "Walk It Out" by

_____

_____

_____

_____

Go continued

Come back together as a group.

》 **Hold your coin. Think of it as the responsibility God has entrusted you with—no matter what that looks like right now. Take a minute to silently ask God to help you value what he has trusted you with and to help you recognize the value he has placed upon others through the responsibilities he has given them.**

After a minute of silence, close your group time in prayer.

prayer⊙

》 **God, thank you for raising each of us up and trusting us to represent you in our churches, our homes, our workplaces, and our relationships—even if we can't understand why you *would*. We also thank you for the leaders you've given us. Help us honor and trust their judgment, knowing that they're accountable to *you,* not to us. Help us trust you in the circumstances you've placed us in and let you lead all of us in the way you see fit. In Jesus' name, amen.**

Go Deeper

To dig deeper into recognizing and honoring the authorities God has placed in our lives, as well as the authority God has already entrusted to us, here are some great resources:

Descending into Greatness by Bill Hybels and Rob Wilkins (Zondervan)

The Heart of a Servant Leader: Letters from Jack Miller by C. John Miller (P & R Publishing)

Spiritual Authority by Watchman Nee (Christian Fellowship Publishers)

Spiritual Leadership by J. Oswald Sanders (Moody)

Is this an area where you'd like to see *us* dig deeper and create more resources? Do you have a great idea we ought to consider? Let us know at info@group.com. We'd love to hear what you're thinking.

Locating the Body

> *But our bodies have many parts, and God has put each part just where he wants it"* (1 CORINTHIANS 12:18).

In this session, we'll journey...

from ⟶ **to**

seeing the connection between knowing our teams and growing our teams...

recognizing and affirming the gifts, skills, and life experiences of those God has placed in our lives.

Before gathering, make sure you have...

○ name tags and pens or markers for everyone

○ background music✶

Optional activities (choose one or both):

Seek and Find

○ **Option A:** Discussion of background music (see page 32)

○ **Option B:** DVD of *Apollo 13* (see page 37)

✶See **Leader Notes,** page 156, for details.

Come and See

(about 15 minutes)

Have your music playing as everyone enters. Give each person a name tag, and make sure everyone has something to write with (but don't let people write yet).

» **Since today's session focuses on teamwork, let's jump right in. Please get into your groups from last week.** (Give groups time to re-form. Assign any new people to groups.) **Hopefully you know each other's first and last names by now. If not, you will by the time we're done.**

You've each been given a name tag. Your fellow group members will help you write on them, and you'll each play a different role in doing that. Follow along with me as we look at the rules together:

- **One person in your group will draw only vertical lines. (For example, the letters "b," "d," "h," and "k" all have vertical lines—but again, that person can draw *only* the vertical lines.)**

- **Another person will draw only horizontal lines (examples: "e," "f," "t," and "z").**

- **Another will draw only curves or circles. (OK, he or she can dot "i"s, too.) (The letters "c" and "e" have curves, and "b" and of course "o" contain circles.)**

- **And one person will draw only angled lines. (For example, "k," "v," "w," or "y" all have angled lines.)**

Take a few moments to decide which group member will take which role, and then I'll tell you what to do next.

If you have groups of three, let one person draw both horizontal and angled lines. For a group of five, have separate people draw curves and circles (and let your circle person dot the "i"s). Wait until you've got everyone's attention again before moving on.

» **Go ahead and start your own name tag, doing only *your* piece. Use both your first and last names. When you're**

> *The capacity to appreciate the gifts of widely varying kinds of workers, and then to help them along the lines of their own personalities and workings, is the main quality for oversight in a mission such as ours.*
>
> —D.E. Hoste

Come and See

◎ What part of this task challenged you the most?

◎ When have you seen people of different gifts, skills, or backgrounds work together to accomplish something bigger than any one of them could accomplish? How did this sense of teamwork affect the people involved? How did it affect the end result?

◎ On the other hand, when have you seen plenty of talent in the room but no teamwork? What happened *then*? What *could* have happened if everyone had worked together?

done, pass your tag to the person on your right, and keep going until everyone's name tag is complete. When you're ready, put your name tags on. Then discuss these questions:

Come back together as a group after 10 minutes. Share highlights and insights from your discussion time.

》 One tricky thing about leadership is…well, *somebody* has to be the leader. At the same time, you're still a *member* of the team you're leading. You don't get to completely separate the two. And it can be difficult to balance your responsibility to get the job done with the responsibilities you have to help others develop as unique people with unique gifts.

But there's good news: These *aren't* two completely separate things. The people God has given you to work alongside are the same people God wants to empower to fulfill his purposes—to complete that bigger picture you're responsible for. It's not just *your* job. So let's get a better understanding of how God wants to guide and lead those he's put you with, and how all of you can serve God *and* each other better.

Seek and Find

(about 20 minutes)

> *Wherever Christ is and wherever we are joined to him, there truly is the intentional, disciplined and faithful ministry of the church. It is not our ministries that make Christ present; it is the present, living Christ who makes our ministries possible.*
>
> —Andrew Purves, The Crucifixion of Ministry

》 The Bible reminds us that we're *all* part of the body of Christ. Let's see what the body looks like on a smaller level—with those teams, those "little bodies," most of us deal with every day. And let's not restrict ourselves to ministry situations; let's apply this idea to any teams God might have us in charge of. Would a couple of volunteers please read Romans 12:3-11 and 1 Corinthians 12:14-27?

After your volunteers read, discuss: ————————————————

If you chose **Option A**, *read on.*
If you're doing **Option B**, *go to page 37.*

》 Before going on, let's stop and appreciate the music that's playing. Take 30 seconds to be still and listen for the different instruments. Close your eyes, if you wish.

You may need to turn your music up for this part of the session. After 30 seconds, discuss: ————————————————

Seek and Find

 Romans 12:3-11; 1 Corinthians 12:14-27

◎ What attitudes, good or bad, can we take toward our roles or abilities, according to these passages?

◎ Which of these attitudes do you struggle with most? Why?

◎ What would "measuring yourselves by the faith God has given us" (Romans 12:3) look like in your own life? How would it change the way you measure yourself and others you work with?

◎ What can make it difficult for you to believe that "God has put each part just where he wants it" (1 Corinthians 12:18)?

◎ How is our music an example of being a body with many different parts?

◎ How do our attitudes affect how well we perform, both together and as individuals?

Go

(about 25 minutes)

》 Get back into your groups. Let someone else in your group lead this next section. Take 15 minutes to read Ephesians 4:1-8 and discuss the following questions together: _____

Come back together after 15 minutes, keeping people with their groups. Ask for volunteers to share highlights and insights from their discussion time. Then have groups move on to Walk It Out.

Walk It Out (about 5 minutes)

Get back into your groups. Let someone who hasn't led yet lead this piece.

How does what you've learned today apply to where you're at right now? How can you put it into practice? Take five minutes in your groups to write one thing you'll do this week to make today's lesson more real in your own life. Share your choices with your group, and make plans to connect before the next session to check in and encourage one another.

✝ **Ephesians 4:1-8**

◉ Who has a "special gift" that corresponds with your special "fault"—that is, who's stronger in an area in which you're weaker? Do you normally seek that person's help? or run the other way? Why?

◉ Think again about the teams you're already on. Who are the ones on *those* teams with gifts that complement one another—even if they don't realize it? How could you help them appreciate each other more?

◉ Who brings out the best in you (or has done so in the past)? What is it about that person that inspires, challenges, or provokes you into giving your best?

◉ How might God use you to bring out the best in someone else you work with—even (or especially) if that person is built differently than you are?

Because God has brought together the people I work with for *his* good, I'll "Walk It Out" by

_____

_____

_____

_____

Go continued

prayer⊙

Come back together as a group. Thank God for the people who have been placed in your lives—in your ministries, your workplaces, your families—and for those you're studying with during this season. Ask God to show you how to bring out the best in every one of those people, even if you can't understand what makes them tick. Ask for the Spirit's help and insight to know the right things to say and do for each person God has placed in your life, so that you work together to accomplish *God's* purposes.

SEEING IT DIFFERENTLY
Seek and Find–Option B

LEADER   *To prompt your group to think about a session in a fresh way, we'll occasionally recommend video clips that your group can enjoy in place of (or in addition to) another part of the session. You'll be surprised by how effectively movies can portray eternal truths, or at least point toward them.*

Instead of the discussion of background music, watch a scene from the movie *Apollo 13*. Astronauts Jim Lovell, Fred Haise, and Jack Swigert "have a problem"—several, in fact. Their scheduled landing on the moon has been scrapped; no one is sure they'll make it back to earth alive; and we've just learned that they're slowly being poisoned by the heightened levels of carbon dioxide they're breathing. Enter Houston's ground crew. Cue the movie to 1:19:57 (DVD Chapter 35), at "Gene, we have a situation…" Stop the clip at 1:21:00 as the ground-crew members each grab an item and we overhear, "Better get some coffee going, too, someone."

GROUP

◎ When has a group or team you've been involved with had to deal with putting a square peg in a round hole…rapidly?

◎ How did you respond? "We gotta come through…get some coffee going"? "We can't do it"? Or some other way? Explain.

◎ How do our attitudes affect how we perform, both together and as individuals?

Move on to Go

Go Deeper

To dig deeper into what it takes to know and grow your teams, here are some great resources:

The Equipping Church by Sue Mallory (Zondervan)

Church Is a Team Sport: A Championship Strategy for Doing Ministry Together by Jim Putman (Baker)

Leading the Team-Based Church: How Pastors and Church Staffs Can Grow Together into a Powerful Fellowship of Leaders by George Cladis (Jossey-Bass)

Transform Your Church with Ministry Teams by E. Stanley Ott (Eerdmans)

Getting Healthy Together

Let us hold tightly without wavering to the hope we affirm, for God can be trusted to keep his promise. Let us think of ways to motivate one another to acts of love and good works" (HEBREWS 10:23-24).

In this session, we'll journey...

from ⎯⎯⎯⎯⎯⎯⎯⎯⎯⎯⎯⎯⎯⎯⎯⎯→ **to**
appreciating how every member   discovering how we can help
of our team keeps a ministry   each other get even healthier.
healthy...

Before gathering, make sure you have...

- ○ blindfold for each group ✴
- ○ enough room in your meeting area ✴
- ○ white board or blackboard

✴See **Leader Notes,** page 157, for details.

Come and See

(about 15 minutes)

>> Last week we explored how we're all members of the body of Christ and we all have our parts to play within it. Let's take one more look at that idea before moving forward today. Get into your groups. (Pause for people to find their groups.)

Think about a time your *physical* body wasn't healthy. For example, maybe you had a major illness, or you broke a bone (or several). In your groups, take five minutes to talk about that. Each of you share about your situation, and then discuss these questions:

> The church has a place in creating healthy, transformed communities. Churches don't have the luxury of withdrawing from the community. Whether they feel wanted or not, churches must realize that the community cannot be healthy... without their active engagement and involvement in its life—that's the way God designed it.
>
> —Rick Rusaw and Eric Swanson, The Externally Focused Church

After five minutes, regain everyone's attention, keeping people with their groups. Share highlights and insights from the discussion time.

>> Let's also take one more look at a passage we explored last week to bring this discussion back into context. Would someone please read aloud 1 Corinthians 12:22-27?

So far, we've talked about leadership in broader terms—that is, not only in church but also in other venues where we lead or are led. This session, we're going to sharpen our focus and explore what a healthy *ministry* looks like and how the ministries *you're* involved in should function. Maybe you're leading a ministry right now, or maybe not, but we'll assume you're involved *somewhere* right now. Wherever and however you're involved, you want your team and your ministry to be healthy. When you're healthy and working together, the effects can reach far beyond *your* team and *your* ministry.

◎ What "normal" things were you unable to do during that time—or unable to do without someone's help?

◎ How did your illness/injury affect others and *their* normal routines?

 1 Corinthians 12:22-27

◎ When have you seen a church or ministry rally around and "pick up" someone who was hurting—physically or any other way?

◎ How did that experience affect that person? your church or ministry? *you?*

When one part of your team suffers or isn't functioning correctly, everyone's affected. But God can use that to do something even more powerful. We're never in this alone, and no matter how much responsibility comes to us, we can always play a part in helping others on our team get stronger—and in helping them *until* they get stronger. Let's look into that more right now.

Seek and Find

(about 20 minutes)

》 Let another person in your group lead this next section. Take 15 minutes to read the following passages in your groups, and then discuss these questions: ————————————————

- 2 Corinthians 6:3–13
- Ephesians 4:11–16
- Philippians 1:29–2:11
- Philippians 2:12–18
- Colossians 3:12–17

After 15 minutes, regain everyone's attention, keeping people with their groups. Share highlights and insights from your discussion time. Let each group leader for this section present his or her group's answer to that final question, and write the group leaders' answers on your white board.

》 It's clear we all need each other. It also can be tough to need each other. Let's try something that will help us see that better—or rather, in this case, *not* see.

**2 Corinthians 6:3-13; Ephesians 4:11-16;
Philippians 1:29–2:11; Philippians 2:12-18; Colossians 3:12-17**

◎ What does it take to serve alongside others—particularly other
Christians—according to these passages? What does it look like in
practice?

◎ Which of these comes easiest to you? Which is hardest? Why?

◎ Putting all this together, what *does* a healthy ministry or team look like?
Come up with a concise one- or two-sentence answer as a group.

Go

(about 25 minutes)

Give each group a blindfold, and ask groups to gather in different parts of your meeting area, as far away from their seats as possible.

》 **You'll each need a volunteer from your group. Go ahead and blindfold that person.** (Pause for volunteers to be blindfolded.) **Now, the rest of you will lead your blindfolded teammate to the other side of the room and back to his or her seat. You can use only your voices to guide your teammate. No touching—just talking.**

That said, you have some choices to make here. You can work together to guide your fellow group member safely to his or her destination. You can guide him or her somewhere *else*. Or you can all give conflicting directions, and let your blindfolded person decide who's right. You don't want to do anything that might hurt your blindfolded person; still, you *could* make things difficult for him or her. *If* you want. Your call.

Ready? Go!

Take up to five minutes for this activity, letting other group members take turns as time allows. Then sit down together, and discuss these questions with the full group:

◎ Those of you who were blindfolded, how did you feel as you were led across the room? Did you have any doubts about how you were being guided? Why or why not?

◎ When have you felt like you were walking blind in a group—like everyone but you knew what was going on? Or like *none* of you knew what was going on? Talk about it.

◎ What were you telling God during that time in your life?

Go continued

Ask for volunteers to read Proverbs 3:5-8 and Hebrews 10:21-25. Then discuss the questions: ——————————————

prayer⟶   Come back together as a group.

Before your closing prayer time, we'd suggest this: Whether or not you do a regular worship time together as a group, have a brief time of singing. Reread Colossians 3:16, and worship together, with or without instruments. Whatever kind of worship music fits your group, join together and sing it. Build up one another's spirits with your voices.

When you're done, thank God again for the people he's put you with—both here and elsewhere. Pray for the service you're all currently doing, and ask God to give each of you the wisdom to see how you can help make the ministries and the teams you're serving God with even stronger.

Walk It Out (about 5 minutes)

Get back into your groups. Let someone who hasn't led yet lead this piece.

How does what you've learned today apply to where you're at right now? How can you put it into practice? Take five minutes in your groups to write one thing you'll do this week to make today's lesson more real in your own life. Share your choices with your group, and make plans to connect before the next session to check in and encourage one another.

✝ Proverbs 3:5-8; Hebrews 10:21-25

◎ What's the connection between trusting God and trusting those you serve God *with*?

◎ How can you connect in more effective ways with your fellow servants of God? How can you make those connections even stronger in the days to come?

Because a healthy team means trusting both others and the God who put us all together, I'll "Walk It Out" by

_____

_____

_____

_____

_____

Go Deeper

To dig deeper into trusting God with your ministry and your team, here are some great resources:

Growing Dynamic Teams (Group)

Doing Church as a Team: The Miracle of Teamwork and How It Transforms Churches by Wayne Cordeiro (Regal)

Made for a Mission by David A. Posthuma (Xulon)

Organic Leadership: Leading Naturally Right Where You Are by Neil Cole (Baker)

The Crucifixion of Ministry: Surrendering Our Ambitions to the Service of Christ by Andrew Purves (IVP)

Making What You Know...Known

"*Now you are my friends, since I have told you everything the Father told me*" (JOHN 15:15b).

In this session, we'll journey...

from ——————————→ **to**
understanding the importance of...well, *understanding* one another...

discovering what keeps us from communicating better and addressing it.

Before gathering, make sure you have...

Optional activities (choose one or both):

Come and See

○ **Option A:** Discussion (see page 50)

   ○ white board, blackboard, or newsprint✳

○ **Option B:** video clip of the classic "Who's on First?" by Abbott and Costello (see page 56)

Go

○ **Option A:** Discussion (see page 54)

○ **Option B:** DVD of *The Village* (see page 57)

✳See **Leader Notes,** page 157, for details.

Come and See

(about 15 minutes)

> Words are for others, not for ourselves; nor for God, who hears not as bodies do, but as spirits should. If we would know this dialect we must learn of the divine principle in us. As we hear the dictates of that, so does God hear us.
>
> —William Penn

If you chose **Option A**, *read on.*
If you're doing **Option B**, *go to page 56.*

Have people get into their groups.

» **In your groups, take turns reading the sentence on our board. The first person should emphasize the first word in the sentence, the second person should emphasize the second word, and so on. Keep going until you've tried all six versions. Then take 10 minutes to discuss these questions together:** ———

After 10 minutes, bring everyone back together to share highlights and insights from the discussion time.

» **We all want to be understood. In truth, if we ever want to accomplish anything together, we *need* to be understood. But sometimes our words and our actions get misinterpreted. And sometimes we really *haven't* fully communicated what's in our heads and hearts, even when we think we have. We can play something back in our own heads dozens of times, and still find that the person standing in front of us has not grasped, or even heard, it *once*.**

So let's examine what good communication looks like, especially in leadership, and how we can do it better.

◎ What different meanings did you get out of this one sentence?

◎ What causes your words to get misinterpreted? What helps people "get" what you're saying?

◎ How do you respond when others misunderstand what you say? How does your response change when the misunderstanding involves people close to you?

Seek and Find

(about 25 minutes)

》 Let's look at one example of a leader communicating to his co-workers in the faith and then break it down a little more. Would someone please read 2 Corinthians 1:3-14? ————————————

After 15 minutes, regain everyone's attention, keeping people with their groups. Share highlights and insights from your discussion time. Let each group leader for this section present his or her group's answer to that final question, and write the group leaders' answers on your white board.

Have another volunteer read John 15:11-15. Then discuss: ————

2 Corinthians 1:3-14

◎ What is Paul trying to say to the Corinthian church in this passage?

◎ What doesn't he express here that he clearly *could* have, and why do you think he doesn't?

◎ How did knowing it was *God's* message affect what Paul was saying?

◎ How would our own speech change if we were more conscious of representing *God?*

 John 15:11-15

◎ What things do we enjoy telling our friends? Why don't we share those things as often with other people?

◎ If we're all Jesus' friends, what keeps us from sharing with other Christians—Jesus' other friends—what Jesus has shared with us?

Go

(about 20 minutes)

If you chose to do **Option A**, *read on.*
If you're doing **Option B**, *go to page 57.*

》 Get into your groups. (Pause.)

Read 1 John 4:17-21, and then discuss the questions on your group page. When you're done discussing, close in prayer with your group instead of doing the normal Walk It Out. Use your prayer time as an opportunity to be open about what you're each facing right now—and to be honest with one another about what each other's next steps might be. Speak the truth in love. Listen to each other without reacting. Then give it all to God. Ask God to open each of you up, and to open up the lines of communication with those you're struggling to get through to right now.

When you're done praying, you're free to go [or hang out, if you're in a small group].

1 John 4:17-21

◎ In what ways does fear stop us from communicating with others—even other Christians—who *need* to know what we're not sharing? How do we show a lack of love when we hold back?

◎ What things do we often do instead of communicating openly?

◎ When *should* we hold back information or feelings, even when it involves something important?

◎ What situation are you facing right now that requires you to step out of your comfort zone—say it: *past your fear*—and communicate with someone more openly and directly? Talk about it.

SEEING IT DIFFERENTLY
Come and See–Option B

LEADER   That's right: For this session, you get *two* video alternatives. Use one, both, or neither—it's up to you.

Instead of the white board activity, keep everyone together to watch a classic clip from the 1945 movie *The Naughty Nineties,* with the comedy team of (Bud) Abbott and (Lou) Costello. If you have computer access, you can easily find the clip on YouTube or other online video sites by searching for "Who's on First." It's also available on various DVDs; if you use *Abbott & Costello: Funniest Routines, Vol. 1,* cue the DVD to 1:10:52 (DVD Chapter 13) and let it run until 1:18:03, when the routine ends. It's a longer clip than normal (more than seven minutes), but you'll get the point and have a good laugh.

GROUP

◎ When have you felt like either Abbott *or* Costello here?

◎ What causes our words to get misinterpreted? What helps people "get" what you're saying?

◎ How do you respond when others misunderstand what you say? How does your response change when the misunderstanding involves people close to you?

Pick up the end of Come and See, with the statement that begins, **"We all want to be understood..."**

SEEING IT DIFFERENTLY
Go—Option B

LEADER   Keep everyone together to watch a scene from the 2004 movie
The Village. The movie takes place in what appears to be an isolated 18th-century
Pennsylvania village, and in this scene we begin to learn what the villagers
believe about the outside world. Cue the movie to 5:00 (DVD Chapter 2), as
the two young women are sweeping. Stop the clip at 7:40, as Mr. Walker asks the
school kids, "Why would they do this?"

GROUP

◎ How would you describe the atmosphere during these scenes?

◎ How does *not* speaking of "those we don't speak of"—whether a person or a
situation—make things bigger instead of smaller?

Ask for a volunteer to read 1 John 4:17-18. Then discuss the questions:

GROUP

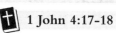

◎ In what ways does fear prevent us from communicating with others? How do
we show a lack of love when we don't communicate?

◎ What's the thing "we don't speak of" in your life right now? Who needs to hear it?
(If it's a sensitive or private situation, share only as much as is appropriate.)

Get into your groups. But instead of your normal Walk It Out time, close
in prayer together. Use your prayer time as an opportunity to be open
about what you're each facing in this area right now—and to be honest
with one another about what each other's next steps might be. Speak
the truth in love. Listen to each other without reacting. Then lift it all up
to God. Ask God to open each of you and open up the lines of communication with those you're struggling to get through to right now.

When you're done praying, you're free to go [or hang out, if you're in a
small group].

Go Deeper

To dig deeper into communicating openly, here are some great resources:

Communicating for a Change: Seven Keys to Irresistible Communication by Andy Stanley and Lane Jones (Multnomah)

Instruments in the Redeemer's Hands: People in Need of Change Helping People in Need of Change by Paul David Tripp (P & R)

Communication and Conflict Management: In Churches and Christian Organizations by Kenneth O. Gangel and Samuel L. Canine (Wipf & Stock)

Leading Out Loud: Inspiring Change Through Authentic Communication by Terry Pearce (Jossey-Bass)

Leading the
~~Change~~ Charge

But forget all that—it is nothing compared to what I am going to do.
For I am about to do something new. See, I have already begun!
Do you not see it?" (ISAIAH 43:18-19a).

In this session, we'll journey...

from ⟶ **to**
understanding that leading
means helping others (and
ourselves) change...

investigating where change is
needed and how we can share
the vision and ownership.

Before gathering, make sure you have...

...well, let's not talk about that *here*. See the Leader Notes on page 158. (And only your *group* leader—the
rest of you leaders need to just wait for it.)

Optional activities (choose one or both):

Go

○ **Option A:** Scripture reading and discussion
(see page 64)

○ **Option B:** DVD of *Hoosiers* (see page 67)

Come and See

(about 10 minutes)

》 **I've got a valuable piece of advice, and I'll share it with you if you give me a dollar. I won't give your dollar back, but trust me, it's worth it. Who's willing to take me up on this?**

Wait for responses, and then ask this question: ———————

If someone's willing to take your offer, thank him or her for the dollar. If you're standing in front of your group, let your volunteer stand with you. Hand that person your slip of paper, and let him or her read it aloud. Keep your volunteer up with you as you discuss the next question: ———————

Leader: Follow through on the plan described in the Leader Notes. Then continue the discussion: ———————

》 **In our last session, we looked at the importance of communicating well, even when it's difficult or uncomfortable. Now we come to the place where we *need* to communicate. When God calls us to take the lead, God wants us to lead people *somewhere.* To do that, we also have to *leave* somewhere. It's our job to help those we lead get from here to there—and then, when we've got them there, to get ready to lead them to the next place.**

Helping people let go of where they're at and embrace what's ahead is a huge part of leadership. And since we're leading, *we're* the first people who need to let go and look forward. So let's get started.

> *Problems are only opportunities in work clothes.*
>
> *—Henry J. Kaiser*

◎ Why are you reacting the way you are right now?

◎ What's one small positive change you'd like to make in your life right now? What would you need to give up? What would the benefits be?

◎ Why did the rest of you hold back?

◎ How is that like the way we normally look at change—even changes we know are positive?

Seek and Find

(about 25 minutes)

Ask for a volunteer to read Matthew 9:14-17. Then discuss these questions: ——————————————

》 Let's apply what Jesus said to other situations where we need "new wineskins." Think about a situation you're involved in right now that you *know* needs changing, and let's start talking it through. ——————

Ask for another volunteer to read Galatians 1:10-24, and then discuss these questions: ——————————————

Matthew 9:14–17

◎ What's the connection Jesus is trying to make between fasting and new wineskins?

◎ Why will the disciples' fasting be different from that of the Pharisees, when the time *does* come?

◎ What might the new wineskin look like in that situation?

◎ Share about a time you made changes in your life—even if it was scary or painful. Looking back now, would you go back to the way things were? Why or why not?

 Galatians 1:10–24

◎ As you read this passage, what changes did you see in Paul's understanding of who God is and what God really wants?

◎ How does Paul help *us* understand our need for change by sharing this with us?

Go

(about 25 minutes)

If you chose **Option A**, *read on.*
If you're doing **Option B**, *go to page 67.*

>> **In your groups, take 15 minutes to read Isaiah
43:16-21 and Romans 12:1-2, discuss the questions that follow, and then move on to Walk It Out
together. Let's plan to come back together in 20
minutes.** ────────────────────────────

Walk It Out (about 5 minutes)

Let someone who hasn't led yet lead this piece.

How does what you've learned today apply to where you're
at right now? How can you put it into practice? Take five
minutes in your groups to write one thing you'll do this week
to make today's lesson more real in your own life. Share your
choices with your group, and make plans to connect before
the next session to check in and encourage one another.

✝ **Isaiah 43:16-21; Romans 12:1-2**

◎ Why does God tell Israel to forget about being delivered from Egypt (Isaiah 43:18)—even though God's goodness is *worth* remembering?

◎ Likewise, why do you need to be a living sacrifice *before* you can "know God's will for you" (Romans 12:2)?

◎ Think again about your situation that needs changing. What's keeping that change from happening?

◎ What could you gain by making that change? Dream a little as you answer.

◎ Think about your last answer. How can you communicate what you just shared (or at least thought) to those you're leading?

Because leading means changing and helping others change with me, I'll "Walk It Out" by

_____
_____
_____
_____

Go continued

prayer ❯ Come back together as a group. Pray for those areas of change you've shared about today. Pray for God's wisdom and courage—not only for yourself but for those you're leading. Ask the Spirit to give you the right words to share that vision of change and to prepare everyone else's hearts to receive it and to work together to make it real.

Go Deeper

To dig deeper into great examples of how to embrace change, here are some great resources:

An Unstoppable Force: Daring to Become the Church God Had in Mind by Erwin Raphael McManus (Group)

Organic Church: Growing Faith Where Life Happens by Neil Cole (Jossey-Bass)

Outgrowing the Ingrown Church by C. John Miller (Zondervan)

Comeback Churches: How 300 Churches Turned Around and Yours Can, Too by Ed Stetzer and Mike Dodson (B&H)

SEEING IT DIFFERENTLY

Go–Option B

LEADER   Instead of the readings and discussion in Go, keep everyone together to watch a scene from the movie *Hoosiers*. The Hickory Huskers (enrollment 64) are hours away from playing the South Bend Central Mighty Bears (enrollment 2,800) for the Indiana state high school basketball championship. Cue the movie to 1:33:15 (DVD Chapter 31), as the team gets off the bus to enter the Butler University fieldhouse (capacity 15,000), where the game will be played. Stop the clip at 1:35:44, as Coach Dale laughs, "This is *big*."

GROUP

◎ Why did Coach Dale have his team measure the foul line and the basket?

◎ Think again about your situation that needs changing. What things do you need to keep in perspective as you start to make those changes?

◎ What could you potentially gain from those changes? Dream a little as you answer.

◎ Think about your last answer. How can you communicate what you just shared (or at least thought) to those you're leading?

Have people return to their groups and go on to Walk It Out.

I Object!

"*Since God chose you to be the holy people he loves, you must clothe yourselves with tenderhearted mercy, kindness, humility, gentleness, and patience. Make allowance for each other's faults, and forgive anyone who offends you. Remember, the Lord forgave you, so you must forgive others*" (COLOSSIANS 3:12-13).

In this session, we'll journey...

from ————————————————→ **to**

seeing the need to address
disagreement and conflict—even
when we're right (and we *are*
right! *Aren't* we?)...

discovering how to better value
and engage others as we
work through our differences
together.

Before gathering, make sure you have...

 ——○ 1 or more beach balls ✳

✳See **Leader Notes**, page 159, for details.

Come and See

(about 10 minutes)

Follow the instructions in the Leader Notes.

》 Let's take what we just experienced with our beach ball(s) and talk about how it might apply to something that's usually considerably less fun. ————

In our last session, we explored how leadership involves change. And as we discovered, change can be tough, and not just for us. Whenever we try to introduce change, we're almost certainly going to hit resistance. Even if we've done a good job of showing why change is a good thing, there will probably be some people who will be less than enthused about it. Some might have legitimate concerns that they still need to work though—they simply haven't caught the vision yet. Some are gun-shy because they've been burned before. Others will quietly (or not so quietly) drag their feet, hoping that you'll change your mind. And still others might be openly critical, antagonistic, or even hostile.

Guess what? You're still the leader. You still need to deal with it. And you need to deal with it in a way that honors God—and honors those people putting up the resistance. And you might have to do it even though they're not honoring God, or you, with their attitudes and actions.

So let's talk through this one and see how God wants to equip us to grow in this area right now.

> *The primary tool in the devil's box is the wedge.*
>
> —*Greg Ogden,*
> Discipleship
> Essentials

Come and See

◎ How do you usually respond when someone throws *criticism* your way? Let it bounce off you? Send it someone else's way? Duck and avoid it? Catch it and hang on to it? Slam it back at the person who threw it at you? Explain your answer.

◎ Does your reaction change when criticism's coming at you from more than one direction? If so, how?

◎ However you respond, how well does your approach usually work for you? Why?

Seek and Find

(about 35 minutes)

» **Let's start by putting ourselves in the shoes of those who might disagree with us. Because we've all been in *their* places at one time or another. And let's talk about that.** ───────

Let's look at one case study on resolving conflict from the Bible. Can someone read Acts 14:26–15:19?

As our volunteer reads, take note of *all* the players in this conflict, and think about each person's or group's side of things as you listen.

After your volunteer reads, discuss these questions: ───────

◎ When have *you* been in the role of outsider or critic? What finally got you on board (or would have, if you can't think of a positive example)?

 Acts 14:26–15:19

◎ What kinds of reactions do we see in this passage? What motivated each of the players here?

◎ What steps were taken to resolve the conflict? What helped everyone come to a decision and move forward?

◎ It might be easy to simply point to the Pharisee Christians as "the bad guys." But what's a situation where *you'd* raise the red flag and say, "That's wrong, and I'm not going along with it"? What, if anything, could get you to change your mind about it?

Seek and Find continued

》 OK, let's break it up now. Get into your groups. Let the person who's led your group the least amount of times so far lead *this* section. Read Colossians 3:12-17 and 2 Timothy 2:23-26, and then take 15 minutes to discuss these questions: ————————

After 15 minutes, come back together. Share highlights and insights from the discussion time.

> *Do I not destroy my enemies when I make them my friends?*
> —Abraham Lincoln

Seek and Find

 Colossians 3:12-17; 2 Timothy 2:23-26

◎ Without naming names, think of someone you regularly have trouble seeing eye to eye with. How would Paul's advice in these two passages help?

◎ What's one positive thing you could say to that person right now? Better yet: What's one thing that person brings to the table that you don't?

◎ How can you create the opportunity to share what you just said with that person?

Go

(about 20 minutes)

Take 30 seconds to read the quote in the margin, and then discuss these questions:

» **Use your Walk It Out time to discuss what you discovered and committed to today, and then pray together in your groups. Some people simply need more understanding and attention. You may never become good friends with others, but you can still learn to work together. There will also be people who go beyond what we've discussed today; for whatever reason, they're hardened against you or what you're trying to accomplish.**

Reread Colossians 3:12–13.

» **Whatever the situation is, pray together in your groups. Pray for God's wisdom and grace to overwhelm you and those you're struggling with. And if it *is* a relentless situation, where the other person is immovable and/or disrespectful, ask God for his strength in dealing with it. Ask God what he's trying to teach you through this situation, and ask God's help in keeping your eyes on *that* rather than on what's going on right now.**

When you have finished praying together, you're free to leave [or hang out, if you're in a small group].

Walk It Out (about 5 minutes)

In your groups, let someone who hasn't led yet lead this piece.

How does what you've learned today apply to where you're at right now? How can you put it into practice? Take five minutes in your groups to write one thing you'll do this week to make today's lesson more real in your own life. Share your choices with your group, and make plans to connect before the next session to check in and encourage one another.

◎ In addition to divisive issues, what keeps us from finding common ground with others?

◎ How can we show love and respect to others, even if we totally disagree with them?

> *Those who honestly agree with you keep you sane.*
> *Those who honestly disagree with you keep you honest.*
>
> —*Carl Simmons*

Because change brings resistance, I'll "Walk It Out" by

_____

_____

_____

_____

Go Deeper

To dig deeper into how to resolve conflict and deal with resistance, here are some great resources:

The Peacemaker: A Biblical Guide to Resolving Personal Conflict by Ken Sande (Baker)

Thriving through Ministry Conflict: By Understanding Your Red and Blue Zones by James P. Osterhaus, Joseph M. Jurkowski, and Todd A. Hahn (Zondervan)

Leading Congregational Change: A Practical Guide for the Transformational Journey by Jim Herrington, Mike Bonem, and James H. Furr (Jossey-Bass)

Firestorm: Preventing and Overcoming Church Conflicts by Ron Susek (Baker)

Being There

"*We loved you so much that we shared with you not only God's Good News but our own lives, too*" (1 THESSALONIANS 2:8).

In this session, we'll journey...

from ⟶ **to**

learning the importance of valuing people for more than what they do...

discovering how we can share more of our lives with those we serve alongside.

Before gathering, make sure you have...

○ as many elements of the Lord's Supper as you're comfortable using ✳

———————————

✳See **Leader Notes,** page 161, for details.

Come and See

(about 25 minutes)

>> Congratulations! You're halfway through this season! And since we've already covered some tough topics, let's start today by taking a little break. Help yourself to a snack, sit down, and just enjoy talking with each other for a while. You don't even have to get in your groups. Talk to whomever you feel like talking to.

> *Christians...forget that listening can be a greater service than speaking.... [H]e who can no longer listen to his brother will soon be no longer listening to God either; he will be doing nothing but prattle in the presence of God too.*
>
> —Dietrich Bonhoeffer, Life Together

After 10 minutes, regain everyone's attention.

>> Now that you've had a chance to relax and share a bit, let's start our "official" discussion time.

Working together isn't just about working; it's even more about the "together" part. Ministry of any kind ultimately isn't about the task—it's about the people God puts in our path while we're doing the task. As we spend time together, we "catch" things—we learn things from one another—that we might never have discovered if we were just focused on the task or following instructions. And sometimes just being able to trust others helps us discover things about ourselves we wouldn't have discovered otherwise.

If we want people to be involved, then we need to be involved with people. It's that simple, and it's that difficult. So let's learn more about how we can become more engaged in each other's lives.

Come and See

◎ What's one new thing you learned today, as you just sat and talked?

◎ How could that knowledge affect how you relate to, or pray for, those people in the future?

Seek and Find

(about 20 minutes)

Discuss these questions ———————————————————————————

Ask for a volunteer to read Acts 2:42–47.

>> Most of us are familiar with this passage about the early church. It's often held up as a model for how *we* should do church. And yet, this example from God's Word has often intimidated us as much as it has inspired us. So let's take the "spiritual context" out of this passage for a few minutes and see what's left to talk about. ———————————————————

◎ When has God used you to really grow others, whether it was one person or a group? What do you think helped that person or persons grow the most?

 Acts 2:42-47

◎ Which of these activities could anyone do, whether he or she knows Jesus or not?

◎ How does adding Jesus to the mix transform these activities into something more—something that honors God even as we enjoy each other's company?

◎ Think again about the first question—particularly, the activities you *didn't* mention. Do we *always* need to do these other activities to make being together "a God thing"? Why or why not?

GROWING IN LEADERSHIP / SESSION 7   83

Go

(about 25 minutes)

》 Get back with your groups. Take 10 minutes to read 1 Thessalonians 2:7-12 and discuss these questions. ———

After 10 minutes, come back together. Share highlights and insights from your discussion time.

Bring out the elements of the Lord's Supper you'll use for this session.

》 We've shared a lot these first several weeks. So before we go any further into this season, let's celebrate that. Not because we have to, but because it's *worth* celebrating. Instead of our regular Walk It Out time, let's stop and reflect on what God's already done and remember that, because of Jesus, we're all in this together.

One thing I hope you've learned about leadership is that, while the responsibility may fall to you, you're not in this alone. Jesus gave us an example, and he gave us way more than that. He shared all of his life with his followers, and he gave all of his life for every one of us. He left us with the opportunity to remember that because of the life he gave for us, we all have life together in him.

Read 1 Corinthians 11:23-33.

》 Let's take a few minutes to prepare our hearts before we share together. Ask God to remove the roadblocks that stand in the way of a deeper relationship with God and deeper relationships with others. Look up when you're done. And in the spirit of verse 33, let's "wait for each other" before we continue.

After everyone's ready, share your elements together. Close in prayer.

prayer⊙ 》 Lord, we thank you for every person here and what each person brings to this group. We also thank you for those people we serve alongside. Bring to our paths even more people whom we can encourage and who can encourage us, as we serve you together. In Jesus' name, amen.

Remind group members to follow up with each other during the week about what they shared together during Go.

1 Thessalonians 2:7-12

◎ In what ways did Paul and company care for and grow the Thessalonian church? What actions and attitudes do you see here?

◎ What kind of "children" do you work with right now? Are they compliant? mischievous? rebellious? something else?

◎ How can you convey to them "I'm in all the way"—that you're there for them not just as a co-worker but as a friend, a fellow "child," maybe even as a "parent"?

Walk It Out (about 5 minutes)

Because we serve people rather than just complete tasks, I'll "Walk It Out" by

_____

_____

_____

Go Deeper

To learn more about how we can invest in each other's lives, here are some great resources:

Growing Out: From Disciples to Disciplers, Season Four: Growing Others by Carl Simmons (Group)

Sacred Companions: The Gift of Spiritual Friendship & Direction by David G. Benner (InterVarsity)

Making Room for Life: Trading Chaotic Lifestyles for Connected Relationships by Randy Frazee (Zondervan)

Organic Church: Growing Faith Where Life Happens by Neil Cole (Jossey-Bass)

Life Together by Dietrich Bonhoeffer (HarperOne)

There When You Need It

'Here, show me the coin used for the tax.' When they handed him a Roman coin, he asked, 'Whose picture and title are stamped on it?'

'Caesar's,' they replied.

'Well, then,' he said, 'give to Caesar what belongs to Caesar, and give to God what belongs to God.'

His reply amazed them, and they went away" (MATTHEW 22:19-22).

In this session, we'll journey...

from ————————————————→ **to**
understanding the value (and quantity!) of the teachable moments God provides...

training our eyes to see and apply them, to others *and* ourselves, as God presents them.

Before gathering, make sure you have...

○ white board or blackboard

Optional activities (choose one or both):

Go

○ **Option A:** Food and discussion (see page 92)

 ○ Food that's served as pieces of a whole, such as pie or a casserole✳

○ **Option B:** DVD of *The Lion King* (see page 96)✳

✳See **Leader Notes**, page 162, for details.

Come and See

(about 10 minutes)

》 Think about a time God used a circumstance to totally surprise you, one that either taught you something totally new or reminded you of something important you'd forgotten. (Pause.) **Now, let's talk about it:** ————————————————————

》 **Last week we explored the importance of being there for your teammates in ministry. This week, we'll build on that and look at one of the more overlooked benefits of spending time with others.**

Think about this: You're going along, growing relationships with those you serve alongside, and a situation just...presents itself. You weren't looking for it. You may not even have felt ready for it. But there it is. God has thrown it across your path anyway.

The good news is, God always does this for a reason. He's providing an opportunity to grow both you and those you're with, and you didn't even have to work for it. But will you recognize that moment when it comes? And how will you let God use it?

So let's begin to take a little of the mystery out of these "God sightings" and see how God might want us to turn those sightings into teachable moments— not only the moments that allow you to teach others, but also the moments God uses to teach _you_.

◎ When has God totally surprised you? What was it that God did or provided?

◎ What did you learn from it?

Seek and Find

(about 30 minutes)

>> **Get into your groups.** (Pause.)

Jesus took advantage of teachable moments all the time, and sometimes he even went out of his way to create those moments. We might think we're just not that creative. And Jesus is...well, you know...*Jesus*. But God often throws things in our paths that we weren't expecting so that he can teach us something new, or teach us something we *thought* we already knew in a brand-new way.

So let's focus on several passages that show Jesus taking whatever's thrown at him—very human situations—and turning them into eternal lessons. And just to prove that this isn't only Jesus' territory, we'll look at one example from Paul's life, too. Read the list of passages, and then discuss the questions that follow. We'll come back together in 15 minutes. ──

[W]e are not to 'catastrophize' and declare the 'end of the world' when things happen. We are to see every event as an occasion in which the competence and faithfulness of God will be confirmed to us.

—Dallas Willard, The Divine Conspiracy

- Matthew 22:15-22
- Mark 12:41-44
- John 8:1-11
- Mark 9:33-37
- Luke 7:36-50
- Acts 17:16-34

Gather everyone's attention after 15 minutes, keeping people with their groups. Share highlights and insights from your discussion time. Use your white board to record groups' answers to your second question. Encourage groups to share as many thoughts as possible.

>> **Take a good look at our list.** (Pause.) **Turn back to your group members, and take 10 more minutes to discuss these questions together:** ──

After 10 minutes, regain everyone's attention, again keeping them with their groups.

Seek and Find

 Matthew 22:15-22; Mark 9:33-37; Mark 12:41-44;
Luke 7:36-50; John 8:1-11; Acts 17:16-34

◎ What common themes or circumstances do you see in these situations?

◎ Besides the fact that Jesus is who he is, what prepared him (and Paul) to use those moments when they came his way? Share as many thoughts as you can.

◎ Which of these qualities or ideas could you use the most right now?

◎ Who do you know who excels in those qualities or ideas? What would you like that person to teach *you*?

Go

(about 20 minutes)

If you chose **Option A**, *read on.*
If you're doing **Option B**, *go to page 96.*

》 **So far we've looked at examples of just-in-time teaching. And since you're all either leading or preparing to lead, and you've been watching someone else lead these sessions, you may have learned a little about teaching on the fly just by watching *me.* Let's find out how much.**

Bring out the food you prepared.

》 **The person with the most teaching experience in your group will lead your next discussion, but all of you will get an opportunity to teach. So grab a serving of the food I just brought out. Then sit in your groups, and take a few moments to figure out who your leader will be.**

Give people time to get some food and sit down in their groups.

》 **You'll notice that what we're eating came in one big piece, and yet you're all about to enjoy a piece of it. And with that, I'm going to throw a teaching opportunity your way. In your groups, spend five minutes sharing at least one idea apiece that answers this question:**

> **• What lesson about leadership and teamwork could you teach right now, using this food as your prop?**

Come up with as many ideas as you can in the next five minutes. Go!

After five minutes, come back together, keeping people with their groups. Ask each group to share at least one of its ideas. Then discuss this question: ——————

◎ You've been together several weeks now. How did your time together help your group come up with more ideas than you would have if this had been your first time together?

Go continued

Ask for a volunteer to read 1 Peter 3:15-16. ——————————

Walk It Out (about 5 minutes)

Get back into your groups. Let someone who hasn't led yet lead this piece.

How does what you've learned today apply to where you're at right now? How can you put it into practice? Take five minutes in your groups to write one thing you'll do this week to make today's lesson more real in your own life. Share your choices with your group, and make plans to connect before the next session to check in and encourage each other.

prayer⊙

Come back together as a group. Ask God to open your group members' eyes to the "God sightings" around them and to give all of you a sense of expectation of what God wants to do with those moments in your lives.

1 Peter 3:15-16

◎ How would the attitude Peter describes here increase the number of teachable moments we have with those around us?

◎ How would it increase the number of teachable moments God has with *us*?

Because God wants me to see and use the teachable moments he gives me, I'll "Walk It Out" by

_____
_____
_____
_____
_____

SEEING IT DIFFERENTLY

Go–Option B

LEADER   Instead of sharing food, watch a scene from the movie *The Lion King*. At this point in the movie, Simba (the lion who would be king) still thinks he caused his father's death—and because he ran away in shame, all the other animals think he's dead, too. Cue the movie to 50:37 (DVD Chapter 15), as Simba burps. But don't start it yet.

》 All four characters in this scene are presented with some kind of teachable moment, and each reacts *very* differently to it. Pay special attention to those reactions as you watch.

Start the clip, and then stop it at 53:43, after Rafiki says, "It is time." Then discuss:

GROUP

◎ What are the different reactions you see here?

◎ Which character are you most like in this scene? Why?

Pick up at the reading of 1 Peter 3:15-16, on page 94.

Go Deeper

To dig deeper into how to discover and share God in every moment, here are some great resources:

God Sightings: Learning to Experience God Every Day (Group)

Finding the Groove: Composing a Jazz-Shaped Faith by Robert Gelinas (Zondervan)

God Space: Where Spiritual Conversations Happen Naturally by Doug Pollock (Group)

The Practice of the Presence of God by Brother Lawrence (Xulon)

Passing the Baton

But you must remain faithful to the things you have been taught. You know they are true, for you know you can trust those who taught you" (2 TIMOTHY 3:14).

In this session, we'll journey...

from ⟶ **to**
understanding the need to prepare others for responsibility...
examining ways to encourage them as we're preparing them.

Before gathering, make sure you have...

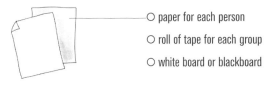

○ paper for each person
○ roll of tape for each group
○ white board or blackboard

See **Leader Notes**, page 162.

Come and See

(about 15 minutes)

》 We'll begin our dash toward the finish line with this session. We'll spend the next *two* sessions, in fact, dealing with what it takes to run *through* the finish line instead of simply stumbling our way to the end. And as with everything else we've learned so far, the answer isn't only about you or me.

So let's jump right in. Would someone please read Exodus 18:13-27?

After your volunteer reads, discuss:

》 Letting go and sharing the load is good advice and good practice. In fact, it's probably the only way those you serve, and serve with, will ever grow. It's often easier said than done, but it's where we need to get to if we expect God's work to grow. God's work *must* become bigger than us.

In this session, we're going to focus more on the preparation part of things, for both ourselves and those we hand responsibilities to. What *can* we prepare to let go of? Who can we begin handing responsibilities to, and how can we prepare them to take what we give them and run with it? Let's begin exploring that now.

Winning is not gathering the largest crowd, but releasing on the world the greatest number of equipped disciples.

—Jim Putman,
"Pastor as Coach"
Rev! Magazine,
November/
December 2008

Exodus 18:13-27

◎ What's the big idea Jethro (Moses' father-in-law) is recommending here? How does his advice help everyone involved?

◎ What smaller tasks does he ask Moses to do, so the big idea here can become a reality?

◎ If Jethro were to make these suggestions about your current commitments, what would he bring up—and how do you think you'd react?

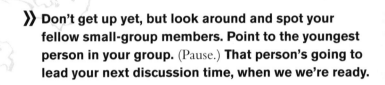

Seek and Find

(about 25 minutes)

>> **Don't get up yet, but look around and spot your fellow small-group members. Point to the youngest person in your group.** (Pause.) **That person's going to lead your next discussion time, when we we're ready.**

Give everyone a piece of paper, and hand a roll of tape to each group leader.

>> **Think of all the commitments you're responsible for in a given week. Take two minutes to list as many of them as you can on your paper.**

If people are still writing after two minutes, regain their attention.

Ask for a volunteer to read Romans 12:4-10, and then discuss: ——————————————————————

>> **Look at your paper again. Which of these responsibilities could you hand off? Be honest. What could you let go of? What could someone else do just as easily as, if not better than, you? Put a check mark next to those items.**

Allow about 30 seconds for people to review and update their lists.

Seek and Find

 Romans 12:4-10

◎ Think about the list you made. How does this passage help us keep "our" work in perspective?

◎ How are we "honoring each other" (verse 10) when we share our load with others? When *wouldn't* we be honoring them by doing so?

Seek and Find continued

>> **Look at your list one more time. Focus on the check marks you made. Who are the people those check marks represent? Take another minute to write their names next to your check marks.**

After another minute has passed,

>> **Roll up your list so you have one long tube, and then tape it. Mark it with something, a symbol or initial, to show it's *your* list.** (Pause.)

OK, *now* get with your groups. But there's one more thing you need to do first. Take your tube, stand it in the palm of your hand, and try to balance it as you get with your fellow group members. If you're already sitting together, get up and change your seats. Go ahead and get started. (Pause.)

Now that you're together, take 10 minutes to discuss these questions: ———————————

After 10 minutes, regain everyone's attention, keeping people with their groups. Share highlights and insights from your discussion time.

◎ How was the balancing act you just did like your ministry—or your life—right now?

◎ How does sharing responsibilities help *you* get back into balance?

Go

(about 20 minutes)

Ask for volunteers to read 2 Timothy 3:10–4:2 and 2 Timothy 4:6–8.

Write everyone's answers on your white board.

》 You're still holding your rolled-up lists. And come to think of it, they look a bit like batons in a relay race, don't they? So go ahead and think of them that way. Turn back to your groups, and pass your batons to your group leader. (Pause.) **Don't open them, leaders; just hang on to them.**

Remember, your lists represent your current responsibilities—including those responsibilities you're handing off in *your* race. Keep that in mind as you discuss the following questions together in your groups. Go on to Walk It Out when you're done discussing. Let's plan to circle back together in 15 minutes for prayer.

Walk It Out (about 5 minutes)

Let someone who hasn't led yet lead this piece.

How does what you've learned today apply to where you're at right now? How can you put it into practice? Take five minutes in your groups to write one thing you'll do this week to make today's lesson more real in your own life. Share your choices with your group, and make plans to connect before the next session to check in and encourage each other.

2 Timothy 3:10–4:2; 4:6-8

◎ How do you see Paul preparing Timothy for leadership here? Come up with as many examples as you can.

◎ What's scariest about handing over (or being handed) this much responsibility?

◎ What's the biggest challenge you face right now in handing things off? How can we make that handoff something we can actually be joyful about? Talk about it, and then write your answers in your Walk It Out section.

> *Trust His tenaciousness, count on His invincibility. Look to Him, and in His time and His way, He will finish the work.*
>
> —Watchman Nee, Changed Into His Likeness

Because handing over responsibility means I let go, I'll "Walk It Out" by

_____

_____

_____

_____

_____

Go _continued_

prayer➌ Come back together as a group. Make sure everyone gets his or her "baton" back. (The markings group members made on the papers earlier should help you identify them quickly.) Have group members hold their batons as you lead in prayer. Ask God to give each person the wisdom to know what to hand off and how and when to do it. Pray that God will give group members confidence and trust in those they give responsibility to and that they'll see the fruits of that trust as they see others growing out.

Go Deeper

To dig deeper into how to prepare others for responsibility, here are some great resources:

Doing Church as a Team: The Miracle of Teamwork and How It Transforms Churches by Wayne Cordeiro (Regal)

The New Breed: Understanding and Equipping the 21st Century Volunteer by Jonathan R. McKee and Thomas W. McKee (Group)

Equipping 101 by John C. Maxwell (Thomas Nelson)

The Volunteer Revolution: Unleashing the Power of Everybody by Bill Hybels (Zondervan)

Learning to Let Go

Give your complete attention to these matters. Throw yourself into your tasks so that everyone will see your progress. Keep a close watch on how you live and on your teaching. Stay true to what is right for the sake of your own salvation and the salvation of those who hear you" (1 TIMOTHY 4:15-16).

In this session, we'll journey...

from ⟶ **to**

exploring how to empower and release others into spiritual leadership...

discovering how we can still be there for them, *without* taking back ownership.

Before gathering, make sure you have...

○ round balloon, *not* inflated, for each group

Optional activities (choose one or both):

Go

○ **Option A:** Discussion of 1 Timothy 1:18-19; 3:14-16 (see page 114)

○ **Option B:** DVD of *Finding Nemo* (see page 118)

See **Leader Notes**, page 162.

Come and See

(about 15 minutes)

>> **Get into your groups. Again, have someone who hasn't recently led your group take charge this time around.** (Pause.)

Give each leader a balloon (still not inflated).

>> **Leaders, here's your mission: Blow up your balloon, and then bat it to your fellow group members, who'll keep it in the air for two minutes.**

One catch, leaders: Once you put the balloon in the air, *you* can't touch it again. Go!

After groups have had two minutes to bat the balloons, regain everyone's attention, keeping people with their groups. Then discuss these questions:

Our task is simply to keep on following, looking only to our Leader who goes on before, taking no notice of ourselves or of what we are doing....then it will seem not extra-ordinary, but quite ordinary and natural.

—Dietrich Bonhoeffer, The Cost of Discipleship

>> **So, here's the second half of the discussion we began last week. Let's assume for a moment that you've already overcome the challenges you talked about in our last session (eventually, you *will*). You've figured out what you can hand off, prepared others to accept those responsibilities, and handed things over to them. Now comes the part that's not so easy for a lot of leaders.**

Once we've given responsibility to someone and seen that the person can handle it, the relationship changes. And that's OK. But we need to change along with the relationship. We need to step back. Not *away*, but back. We need to allow our responsibility to become truly *the other person's* responsibility. In short, we need to learn to let it go.

Come and See

◎ Leaders: What was it like watching your team but not being able to help?

◎ Everyone: In what ways were your leaders still participating?

◎ How is this similar to leadership in your own church right now? your *own* approach to leadership?

Something we always need to keep in mind when we give others responsibilities in God's work, no matter what the responsibilities involve, is that we're not just handing off tasks. And we're not just handing off responsibilities to *them*. It's *God's* work. Ultimately, we're entrusting others to follow *God's* leading to get the work done. And that means trusting those people *to God*. We're asking God to take those people where we can't go, because it's no longer our job. We should still be there to support them, but we now also have to trust them, and trust God, in this process. It's easy on paper but often tough in real life. So let's talk about it.

Seek and Find

→ (about 20 minutes)

》 Turn back to your groups. (Pause)

Before we begin looking at God's Word today, let's try something a bit different. You'll all take a turn giving a blessing to each member of your group. It doesn't have to be profound or wordy. Just acknowledge how you see God working in that person, and ask God to continue to bless the work you're seeing. For example, "Lord, I appreciate how [name] always knows how and when to comfort others. May you continue to bless and help [name] to touch others' lives as [he/she] has touched ours."

Everyone understand? (Pause.) **Let's take five minutes and bless each other's socks off!**

After five minutes, regain everyone's attention, keeping people with their groups. Then discuss: ———————

Ask for a volunteer to read Matthew 3:13-17.

》 We're not Jesus. But as a human, Jesus experienced life and even the same emotions we do. And Scripture reminds us that we, too, are adopted sons and daughters of God (see Romans 8:15). So let's take a few minutes to look at this scene from a more human perspective. ———————

Hearing God's blessing—and knowing we truly have it—changes everything. It changes the way we look at God, the way we look at God's work, the way we look at ourselves, the way we look at others.

Seek and Find

◎ What was it like to be blessed by others? to bless them?

◎ Why don't we bless others more often?

 Matthew 3:13-17

◎ How do the Father and the Spirit empower a human Jesus here?

◎ How do you think you'd be changed if God said this about you, this clearly?

And because we know God and know what it's like to have his blessing, God wants us to extend his blessing to others, especially those God has led us to place our trust in. Our brief time of blessing earlier was just a taste of how God can use us to bless others, even as we're increasing their workload. Let's look at a few more examples today.

Go

(about 20 minutes)

>> In your groups, read 1 Timothy 4:11-16 and 2 Timothy 1:2-8, and then take 10 minutes to discuss these questions:

After 10 minutes, bring everyone back together. Share highlights and insights from the discussion time.

>> We need to give people we're leading the chance to succeed. But equipping them to take responsibility and grow further in the gifts and abilities God has given them is never only about sharing information.

What's even more important is giving them the *confidence* to succeed. We need to let those we're handing responsibility to know we have faith in them. We need to let them know how we're already seeing God working in them. And we need to be very clear in telling them that *we* believe they can do this—especially if *they* don't believe it for themselves yet.

And there's one more part. We need to let them know that we *can't* always be there for them—but Jesus will be there. And that's the most important piece of information we can ever help them understand. And we need to understand it, too, if we really want to fully let go and let God do his work.

1 Timothy 4:11-16; 2 Timothy 1:2-8

◎ In what ways does Paul bless Timothy in these passages? How does he communicate his confidence in Timothy—and in *God's work* in Timothy?

◎ Who needs to hear some of these things right now? What would you say to that person if he or she were here?

Go continued

If you chose **Option A**, *read on.*
If you're doing **Option B**, *go to page 118.*

Ask for volunteers to read 1 Timothy 1:18-19 and 3:14-16. ──

prayer⟿

❯❯ **God has given each of you strengths—and weaknesses. And God uses both for his glory as we give them back to him. And that's true of everyone here today. So I'd like to conclude this lesson with a blessing for all of you. Bow your heads, please.** (Pause.)

May the Lord continue to strengthen each of you where your strength is needed, and to break you where you need to be broken, so that you may see God's strength there as well. May God bless you as you bless others through your words and your actions. May God put in your path people you can trust with God's work, and may you experience God's joy as you let go and watch God work through them.

In Jesus' name, amen.

Walk It Out (about 5 minutes)

Get back into your groups. Let someone who hasn't led yet lead this piece.

How does what you've learned today apply to where you're at right now? How can you put it into practice? Take five minutes in your groups to write one thing you'll do this week to make today's lesson more real in your own life. Share your choices with your group, and make plans to connect before the next session to check in and encourage each other.

1 Timothy 1:18-19; 2 Timothy 3:14-16

◎ How do we strengthen people we care about when we entrust them to Jesus? How does doing that strengthen us?

◎ What or who are *you* still having trouble letting go of?

◎ How will letting it go help both you and everyone else involved grow more fully into whom *God* wants you to be?

Because none of us can go to the next place God wants us to get to without letting go of where we're at, I'll "Walk It Out" by

_____

_____

_____

_____

_____

SEEING IT DIFFERENTLY

 Go–Option B

LEADER Instead of reading the passages in 1 Timothy in Go, watch a scene from the movie *Finding Nemo*. Cue the movie to 9:43 (DVD Chapter 3), as Nemo says, "Dad, you can go now." Stop the clip at 13:26, as Mr. Ray tells the rest of the school, "There's nothing to see; gather over there."

GROUP

◎ How does Marlin overreact here? What legitimate fears does he have?

◎ What or who are *you* still having trouble letting go of?

◎ How will letting it go help you grow more fully into who *God* wants you to be? How will it help everyone else involved?

Go on to Walk It Out.

Go Deeper

To dig deeper into how to hand off leadership—and *keep* your hands off—here are some great resources:

Simply Strategic Volunteers: Empowering People for Ministry by Tony Morgan and Tim Stevens (Group)

The Equipping Church by Sue Mallory (Zondervan)

TransforMissional Coaching: Empowering Leaders in a Changing Ministry World by Steve Ogne and Tim Roehl (B&H)

Unfinished Business: Returning the Ministry to the People of God by Greg Ogden (Zondervan)

Experiencing LeaderShift: Letting Go of Leadership Heresies by Don Cousins (Cook)

Keeping the Fire Lit

"*If you think you are standing strong, be careful not to fall. The temptations in your life are no different from what others experience. And God is faithful. He will not allow the temptation to be more than you can stand. When you are tempted, he will show you a way out so that you can endure*" (1 CORINTHIANS 10:12-13).

In this session, we'll journey...

from ————————————————→ **to**
taking stock of our current   identifying ways we can "stay lit."
spiritual, physical, and emotional
needs...

Before gathering, make sure you have...

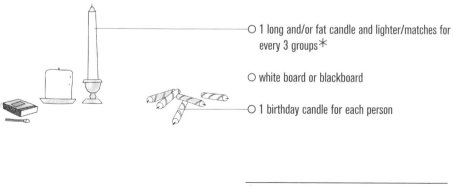

O 1 long and/or fat candle and lighter/matches for every 3 groups ✳

O white board or blackboard

O 1 birthday candle for each person

✳See **Leader Notes,** page 162, for details.

Come and See

(about 15 minutes)

Ask people to stand, gather in their groups, and remain standing. Then ask groups to join two other groups to form larger groups.

》 **Here's how we're going to start today: In your combined groups, two groups will form a corridor, and the third group will try to walk the length of the corridor. Everyone will get a chance, but decide now which groups will form the corridor first and which group will walk through it.**

Pause for groups to organize.

》 **If you're making up the corridor, line up across from each other, and then step back so there's about 6 feet between the two lines.**

If you're in the other group, find the front of the line, and decide which of you will go first.

Allow 30 seconds for groups to get ready. Give the first person in each walking group a lit candle and lighter/matches.

》 **If you're holding a candle, you'll try to walk through our human corridor without having your candle blown out. If your candle goes out, you can relight it and keep walking until you get to the other side or give up and let the next person in line have a try. Those of you forming the corridor can't move or bend toward the candle—no cheating here—but *do* try to blow out the candle as many times as you can.**

> The greatest enemy of intimacy with God is service for God.
>
> —Dallas Willard

Come and See

◎ What were you thinking or feeling as you tried to keep your candle lit?

◎ What did you do to keep your candle from being blown out?

◎ What specific things do you do to keep your life in Jesus from being "blown out"?

Once all groups have had a turn, get into your smaller groups, and take 10 minutes to discuss these questions:

After 10 minutes, come back together. Share highlights and insights from your discussion time.

》 **We need to stay lit in Jesus—and *by* Jesus. As we're doing his work, we often encounter more and more things that can cause us to burn out or drive us into making choices that are less than God's best. That's what we'll deal with in these next two sessions. This week we're going to look at what we need most right now, in order to stay fully alive in Jesus even as we lead.**

Seek and Find

(about 20 minutes)

Discuss these questions together: ———————

Ask for a volunteer to read Luke 4:1–13.

》 **We normally look at these temptations as belonging only to Jesus, at the beginning of *his* earthly ministry. But let's break this down further.** ——————

Write responses on your white board. Put the responses in the appropriate column under the three temptations Satan used to tempt Jesus. Then lead people in discussing this follow-up question together: ——————

Write responses to this question on your white board, too.

》 **Take another look at Jesus and his situation in the beginning of this passage. Forty days is a long time to be hungry and tempted nonstop, after all.** ——————

This is a tough subject, and if you've been in this kind of situation before, you know *how* tough. The good news is, God doesn't leave us here. Let's take some time now to reflect on God's presence and goodness so we can move forward from wherever we are.

◎ On a scale from 1 to 10, with 10 being "fully lit" and 1 being "snuffed out"—how lit up are you right now, really?

◎ How might your current condition be affecting people you're leading? How's their condition affecting *you*?

 Luke 4:1-13

◎ What human needs does Satan appeal to with each of these temptations? Put another way, What's he suggesting he can deliver that God *won't*?

◎ What are some ways we try to "get around God" and meet these needs on our own?

◎ How can our own ability to follow Jesus—and lead others—be compromised or taken off course when our resources are running low?

Go

(about 25 minutes)

》 The temptations and struggles we face as leaders may *look* different from those we faced when we weren't leading, but they're usually the same basic issues. Only the circumstances—and often, the number of others affected or involved—have changed. So let's look back at how God has already carried each of us through our past struggles and maybe get some idea of how God's going to grow us further now.

What mountaintop experiences—times when every-thing went right—have you encountered? What valleys, when *nothing* seemed to go right? How about roller coasters, when "it was the best of times, it was the worst of times"? Or wilderness times, when you just felt dry and empty and maybe couldn't even under-stand why? Take 10 minutes to write a brief description of as many of those experiences as you can remember.

After 10 minutes, gather everyone's attention.

》 Get into your groups. (Pause.) **Read 1 Corinthians 10:12-13, and then discuss the questions. When you're done, go right into Walk It Out. We'll come back for prayer in 15 minutes.**

Walk It Out (about 5 minutes)

How does what you learned today apply to where you're at right now? How can you put it into practice? Take five minutes in your groups to write one thing you'll do this week to make today's lesson more real in your own life. Share your choices with your group, and make plans to connect before the next session to check in and encourage each other.

Mountaintops: Valleys:

Roller coasters: Wilderness times:

✝ 1 Corinthians 10:12-13

◎ What have you learned from your previous times in each of the places you wrote about? How did God teach you to be careful, or show you a way out, in those times?

◎ Which of these places are you closest to being in right now? What may God be trying to remind you about, based on how he's guided you through other times like this?

Because God wants me to stay lit, I'll "Walk It Out" by

_____

_____

_____

_____

Go continued

Come back together as a group. Give everyone a birthday candle.

prayer⊙   »   Before we pray, take note of the section that follows this session, titled "My Spiritual Health Plan." That's your homework this week. You'll notice that many of the questions aren't what we normally consider "spiritual." But God does. God's Spirit needs to be involved in *every* aspect of our lives. We've touched on many of these areas this season, so hopefully you'll already have some answers to start talking over with God. The idea here is to work through a broader and longer-term plan to get more spiritually healthy so that when tough times hit, you've got the reserves you need to stay lit.

Set aside time this week for you and God to work through these questions together. There isn't a single area in your lives where you can't grow, and keep growing, closer to God. Use this time to let God have all of them. Ask God how he wants you to respond to his love and guidance.

You'll need at least an hour to work through this, if you do it right. So do it right. Take every part of your life to God, and let God address all of it, not just the most urgent things or the things *you* think are most important. All right? (Pause.)

So, in closing, let's remember that staying lit isn't just for us. Listen as I read.

Read Philippians 2:14-15.

》 **As we stay lit, God shows his love and his life to others through us. We need to have life in Jesus to be able to share it with others. Let's remember that as we close in prayer.**

To make your prayer time even more special, dim the lights, and have everyone light a birthday candle before you begin praying.

●prayer

》 **Lord, wherever you have us right now, you've put us alongside others who have the opportunity to see you at work within us. Help us to be your lights to this world. If we're on fire for you right now, help us humbly shine our flame so others see it. If we're struggling, help us place our trust and reliance upon you so that we can be refreshed and rekindled—and so others can see that your power and your love are just as available to them.**

We thank you for everything you've already carried us through. Help us to never forget your love and your mercy to us, and to never stop showing it to those around us. In Jesus' name, amen.

Go Deeper

For those wanting to dig deeper into how to stay "lit," here are some great resources:

Simply Relevant: Relational Bible Series for Women— HeartSpa (Group)

Crazy Love: Overwhelmed by a Relentless God by Francis Chan (Cook)

Mad Church Disease: Overcoming the Burnout Epidemic by Anne Jackson (Zondervan)

Fresh Wind, Fresh Fire: What Happens When God's Spirit Invades the Hearts of His People by Jim Cymbala (Zondervan)

Leading on Empty: Refilling Your Tank and Renewing Your Passion by Wayne Cordeiro (Bethany House)

My Spiritual Health Plan

As you read each of these questions, think in terms of where you're generally at right now, not simply where you'd like to be or how you are in your best or worst moments. Answer each question as specifically and concisely as possible.

Once you've written your answer, stop and pray. Invite God into every response you put down. Ask God how to address each issue right now. Who or what could God provide to help you grow? If there's a specific person, write his or her name. If there's a class you could take, a new way of serving others, or books you could read, name them. If there's a specific word you need to hear from God, spell it out—God knows already, but maybe you just need to come out and say it. If there's something you need to let go of, put that down, too. Whatever you believe God's telling you, put it down on paper. And then pray some more.

If any (or even most) of your answers are "I don't know," write *that* down. And then talk to God about that, too.

Good luck. May God bless your time with him beyond what you hope for!

Spiritual Health

MY CHECKUP LIST	MY DIAGNOSIS—AND GOD'S PRESCRIPTION
When do I more fully experience God's love and presence? What's God trying to tell me through that?	
What am I doing right now that I *know* God wants me to do?	
What's one thing about God I'd like to know more about?	
What's one thing I know about God but wish I could truly *experience*?	
What most distracts me from God's presence?	
What's one new thing I'd like God to do in my life?	

General Personal Health

MY CHECKUP LIST	MY DIAGNOSIS—AND GOD'S PRESCRIPTION
What's the most rewarding part of my day? How aware am I of God during that time?	
What takes up more of my time, energy, and resources than it's worth?	
What parts of my personal life aren't getting *enough* attention?	
Who or what do I most neglect at home?	
What gives me so much joy that I really should do it more often? (This doesn't have to be a "spiritual" answer.)	
What areas of my life are overloaded? What can I hand off or just let go of?	
How can I communicate more openly or directly?	
In what areas of my life do I need to become more disciplined?	
In what areas do I most need to "lighten up" and give myself a break?	

Leadership Health

MY CHECKUP LIST	MY DIAGNOSIS—AND GOD'S PRESCRIPTION
What do I enjoy most about leadership?	
What's the hardest thing about leadership for me?	
What area(s) of leadership would I like to learn more about?	
In what area(s) of leadership do I find myself thinking, "I could not care less"—but I know I need to care *more*?	
What's the one thing people ask me for that I have trouble giving?	

Done? Good. Except you're not *quite* done. Look back over what you wrote, and then answer the following two questions:

◎ Out of all the answers you wrote, what would be your top three priorities?

◎ Who specifically can help keep you accountable, connected to Jesus, and growing? (If you think of different people in different areas, write each of their names.)

Leader, Equip Thyself

So I run with purpose in every step. I am not just shadowboxing. I discipline my body like an athlete, training it to do what it should. Otherwise, I fear that after preaching to others I myself might be disqualified" (1 CORINTHIANS 9:26-27).

In this session, we'll journey...

from ⟶ **to**

understanding the need to take care of ourselves *before* we're overwhelmed or burned out...

developing a spiritual health plan so we can stay on track in the long term.

Before gathering, make sure you have...

nothing. Just *be* there!

See **Leader Notes**, page 163.

Come and See

(about 20 minutes)

>> **We're closing in on the finish line for this season, but there's a lot left for us to learn. And today we're going to begin learning *how* we can learn it and why we need to. So let's jump right in.**

Ask for volunteers to read John 15:3-11 and 1 Corinthians 9:24-27, and then discuss: ───────────────────

>> **Without naming names, think of someone who "disqualified" himself or herself in some way, or simply gave out, before his or her "race" was over. Chances are, sadly, it won't take you long.** (Pause.) **Again, without naming names, let's talk about the examples we thought of.** ──────────────

No Bible study can teach you everything. But we want to give you enough equipment so that when this season's done you have what you need to continue walking out the next steps God has placed before you—even the ones you don't know about yet. We want everyone to finish well, and this session's going to help you find some of the tools you need to do that.

Last week, we looked at the struggles we're already facing and how to face them even better with God's help. In this session, we're going to become more proactive in our own spiritual preparation and growth. We'll look at how to be ready *before* we're overtaken by circumstances or simply reacting to what comes our way. How can we build ourselves and each other up, so we're ready for whatever's in store for us next? Let's find out.

> *Everyone thinks of changing humanity and no one thinks of changing himself.*
>
> —Leo Tolstoy

Come and See

 John 15:3-11; 1 Corinthians 9:24-27

◎ Why is staying connected, rather than connecting in starts and stops, so critical to bearing fruit?

◎ What regularly interferes with your connection—and your joy in Jesus?

◎ Looking back now, what were some warning signs that person—or you, on his or her behalf—could have caught earlier?

◎ Even though this is a negative example, what positive lessons have you taken away from it? What do you watch out for now, for yourself or in others?

Seek and Find

(about 30 minutes)

Have people get into their groups.

» Last week, we focused on strengthening those areas where we're most susceptible right now. This week we'll look at how we can become stronger and more mature in *every* area of our lives. Our lives aren't made up of a series of separate compartments; every part affects every other part. When our weaknesses are shored up, we can focus more on our strengths. And even when our strengths give out—because we all have our limits—we're able to draw from where God has strengthened us in other parts of our lives. Let's help each other do that today.

Hopefully, since our last session, each of you has been able to take some time alone with God and examine where you're at right now and where you'd like to be. Today you'll explore your answers in your group.

A leader is a person who has learned to obey a discipline imposed from without, and has then taken on a more rigorous discipline from within.

—J. Oswald Sanders, Spiritual Leadership

Seek and Find

>> Refer to your questions (and answers) in "My Spiritual Health Plan," starting on page 131. As there's a lot to cover here—and you'll run out of time if you try to do everything—focus especially on the answers to your last two questions, on page 135. This time *is* your Walk It Out time today, so you'll have a half-hour to work through this together. Make sure everyone gets time to talk about what God's showing him or her. As a group, talk through what the next steps for each of you might look like.

Let's come back together in 30 minutes. If you have time left over, pray together about what you've shared. Chances are, though, you'll want to keep talking. If that's the case, set aside time this week to do that. Good luck!

Bring everyone back together after 30 minutes. Give groups a heads-up when there are 10, then 5, minutes remaining.

Go

(about 20 minutes)

» I hope your time together has lifted all of you up. Still, you might be reflecting on what God has shown each of you and thinking, How am I going to do all that?

You're not. If there's one thing you take away from this session, let it be this: When God provides the vision, God also provides the means. We simply need to prepare ourselves to receive it. We need to trust God.

Ask for volunteers to read Philippians 4:8-9 and Matthew 6:33. ————————————————————

» Shut your eyes. (Pause.) We're going to close today in prayer. But first, take two minutes to silently ask God to show you at least one thing about himself that's true, honorable, right, pure, lovely, admirable, excellent, and worthy of praise. Silently thank God for it, and ask God to continue revealing more of himself to you.

prayer⊙

After two minutes, close in prayer.

» Lord, we thank you for the things you've revealed to us this past week and over the course of this season. Help us remember that you're always with us, always revealing your goodness to us. Open our eyes and help us see it more. And help us walk out the things you've shown us. Give us the strength, the wisdom, and the friendships to help us walk this out together. In Jesus' name, amen.

Philippians 4:8-9; Matthew 6:33

◎ How does Paul's guidance in Philippians help us live out Jesus' command in Matthew? Explain your answer.

Go Deeper

To dig deeper into developing a long-term spiritual-health plan, here are some great resources:

Spiritual Maturity: Principles of Spiritual Growth for Every Believer by J. Oswald Sanders (Moody Press)

Strengthening the Soul of Your Leadership: Seeking God in the Crucible of Ministry by Ruth Haley Barton (IVP)

Margin: Restoring Emotional, Physical, Financial, and Time Reserves to Overloaded Lives by Richard Swenson (NavPress)

Sacred Companions: The Gift of Spiritual Friendship & Direction by David G. Benner (IVP)

Let My Love Open the Door

A third time he asked him, 'Simon son of John, do you love me?'

"Peter was hurt that Jesus asked the question a third time. He said, 'Lord, you know everything. You know that I love you.'

"Jesus said, 'Then feed my sheep.'...

"Peter asked Jesus, 'What about him, Lord?'

"Jesus replied, 'If I want him to remain alive until I return, what is that to you? As for you, follow me'" (JOHN 21:17, 21-22).

In this session, we'll journey...

from →
looking at where God has taken us this season...

to
exploring where we might be headed next—and how Jesus' love will get us there.

Before gathering, make sure you have...

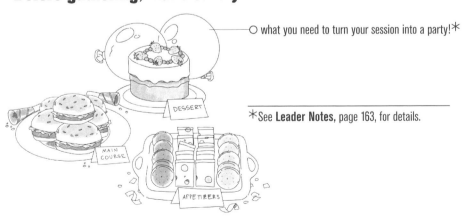

○ what you need to turn your session into a party! ✱

✱See **Leader Notes,** page 163, for details.

Come and See

(about 15 minutes)

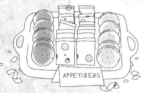

» Well, we've made it. And we've covered a lot of ground this season, so let's reflect once more on where God has taken us. Help yourself to your first course, and then get into your groups.

Before you get comfortable, take a few moments to congratulate one another. Handshakes, backslaps, hugs—whatever works for your group. Take some time to show your appreciation for one another and how far you've come together this season.

Once you're settled back in, take 10 minutes to discuss these questions together: ——————

> *An old leadership adage is relevant to our dilemma: The things that got us to where we are today will not get us to where we need to be tomorrow.*
>
> —George Barna,
> Growing True
> Disciples

After 10 minutes, regain everyone's attention.

» We've spent a lot of time lately examining where we're at with God right now and how he wants to work in us. Today we're going to take one more step outward and consider how God might next want to work through us. What's God preparing us for? What has God put on our minds and hearts, and how have our experiences—both good and bad—prepared us to start living the next steps out?

Let's dream a little today and begin to discover the bigger dreams God might have in store for us. But first, help yourself to the next course. Then we'll sit down and explore God's Word together.

Come and See

◎ What has God shown you this season that has really stuck with you? How have you responded to that so far?

◎ How has this group helped you grow out further? Be specific.

◎ Who in your group would you say radiates God's love the most? Why?

Seek and Find

(about 25 minutes)

Wait until everyone's settled back in before continuing.

» We're going to read a longer passage from the Bible this session. Those of you going on to Season Six of Growing Out (*Growing in Your Mission*) will see this approach a lot more often. We'll look at a "case study" from God's Word to see how others before us have handled walking out the vision God has given them. Then we'll see how it might apply to what God wants to do with the vision and mission he has given each of *us*.

Here, Jesus is preparing to leave this earth, but there's still so much the disciples—especially Peter, in this case—need to understand. And Jesus is about to help them do that. Pay attention to what Jesus says and does, and why. Try to imagine Jesus' "tone" each time.

Ask for a volunteer to read John 21:1-22. Afterward, discuss these questions:

John 21:1-22

◎ What does Jesus do and say to help the disciples understand what's in store for them? How does he reassure them that they'll be able to do it?

◎ Which of these sayings would most apply to what Jesus is showing you right now? Or is Jesus telling you something else (and if so, what)?

◎ Look again at verse 22. Where do *you* need to stop paying so much attention to everyone and everything else and just follow Jesus?

◎ How much do you love Jesus right now—really? Why do you say that?

Go

(about 20 minutes)

DESSERT

≫ **Grab your last course. Then get into your groups one more time and discuss these questions together. When you're done, go on to Walk It Out. Let's plan to come back together in 15 minutes.** ————

Did Moses retire?
Did Paul retire?
Peter? John? Do
military officers retire
in the middle of a
war?

—*Ralph Winter*

Walk It Out (about 5 minutes)

Let someone who hasn't led yet lead this piece.

How does what you've learned today apply to where you're at right now? How can you put it into practice? Take five minutes in your groups to write one thing you'll do this week to make today's lesson more real in your own life. Share your choices with your group, and make plans to connect before the next session to check in and encourage one another.

◎ What's the last great meal you had? How did each course prepare you for the next one?

◎ What "course" do you feel like you're in, in your own life and ministry right now? Why?

✝ Read Romans 8:28-39

◎ One more time: How much do you love Jesus right now—really? What would it take for you to realize how "unseparated" you truly are from Jesus' love?

◎ How will Jesus' love help you move on to the next "course" of your life and ministry?

Because I need to follow Jesus wherever *he* leads, I'll "Walk It Out" by

_____

_____

_____

_____

_____

Go continued

prayer⊙

Come back together as a group.

Keep this one simple and direct. Thank God for all the people in your group and for their leadership wherever God has placed them. If you have a small enough group, use everyone's name. Ask that Jesus' love would become more real to every person— and *through* every person—in your group. And ask God to help each of you overcome anything that stands in the way of experiencing Jesus' love more deeply.

When you're done—and as time allows—let the party continue!

Go Deeper

To dig deeper into how to discover and act on what God has next for you, here are some great resources:

Growing Out: From Disciples to Disciplers, Season Six: Growing in Your Mission by Carl Simmons (Group)

Do Hard Things: A Teenage Rebellion Against Low Expectations by Alex and Brett Harris (Multnomah)

Just Courage: God's Great Expedition for the Restless Christian by Gary A. Haugen (IVP)

The Irresistible Revolution: Living as an Ordinary Radical by Shane Claiborne (Zondervan)

General Tips

- **Read ahead.** Although these sessions are designed to require minimum preparation, read each one ahead of time. Highlight the questions you feel are especially important for your group to spend time on.

- **Preview DVD clips.**

- **Enlist others.** Don't be afraid to ask for volunteers. Who knows? They may want to commit to a role such as teaching a session or bringing snacks once they've tried it. However, give people the option to say, "No, thanks" as well.

- **Be prompt.** Always start on time. If you do this from the beginning, you'll avoid the tendency of group members to arrive later and later as the season goes on.

- **Gather supplies.** Make sure to have the supplies for each session on hand. (All supplies are listed on the opening page of each session.) Feel free to ask other people to help furnish supplies. This will give them even more ownership of the session.

- **Discuss child care.** If you're leading a small group, discuss how to handle child care—not only because it can be a sensitive subject, but also because discussing options will give your group an opportunity to work together *as* a group.

- **Pray anytime.** Be ready and willing to pray at times other than the closing time. Start each session with prayer—let everyone know they're getting "down to business." Be open to other times when prayer is appropriate, such as when someone answers a question and ends up expressing pain or grief over a situation he or she is currently struggling with. Don't save it for the end—stop and pray right there and then.

- **Let others talk.** Try not to have the first or last word on every question (or even most of them). Give everyone an opportunity to participate. At the same time, don't put anyone on the spot—remind people that they can pass on any questions they're not comfortable answering.

- **Stay on track.** There are suggested time limits for each section. Encourage good discussion, but don't be afraid to "rope 'em back in."

- **Hold people accountable.** Don't let your group off the hook with the assignments in the Walk It Out section—this is when group members apply in a personal way what they've learned. Encourage group members to follow through on their assignments.

- **Pray.** Finally, research has shown that the single most important thing a leader can do for a group is to spend time in prayer for group members. So why not take a minute and pray for your group right now?

Session 1

- Read the General Leader Tips starting on page 153, if you haven't already.

- If this is the first time you're meeting as a group, take a few minutes before your session to lay down some ground rules. Here are three important ones:

  1. Don't say anything that will embarrass anyone or violate someone's trust.

  2. Anything shared in the group *stays* in the group, unless the person sharing it says otherwise.

  3. No one has to answer a question he or she is uncomfortable answering.

- We suggest subgroups of four for this season. (If the math doesn't work, three or five people in a group is fine.) This size is a bit less intimate than in past seasons of Growing Out, but there's a reason for that. Leadership involves dealing with multiple personalities, and it isn't always as warm and personal as we might like it to be. But it *can* be. A slightly larger group size will help you to really play with the ideas in this study while keeping things reasonably "safe" and keeping everyone involved. You'll be creating teams of people who'll learn to work together for this entire season, and by doing so, you'll help them grow. And don't be surprised if some great friendships grow out of it, too!

- In this session and the ones to come, we ask group members to take turns leading. That's intentional. Everyone's getting an opportunity to lead. Don't allow participants to fall back on a "he/she's our leader/we're the followers" mentality. Even if groups have a clear leader, use the opportunities we provide to allow God to grow each person in leadership, as people learn and serve together.

- If you're adventurous, extend this principle to the leadership of your sessions as well. Ask a different person to facilitate the session each week. Again, take advantage of this safer environment to get everyone better prepared for leading "out there."

• As you write answers on your white board in Come and See—and in future sessions, too—be sure to thank each person for his or her contribution. Encourage everyone to participate. Be the leader you want each person in your group to become.

• The bowls in the supplies list are there so people won't see what coins they're choosing. Give a bowl to each group, each with a penny, a nickel, a dime, and a quarter. If a group has five people, throw an extra penny in its bowl.

Session 2

• If new people join the group this session, use part of the Come and See time to ask them to introduce themselves to the group, and have people pass around their books to record contact information (page 18). Give a brief summary of the points covered in Session 1.

• If you have newcomers this week, try to create new groups of newcomers, if possible. If you have fewer than three newcomers, spread them out among your existing groups. And while you may not need to worry about it this week, start thinking about this: If all your groups have at least four people and you have at least one group of five when someone new arrives, ask your fivesome and the newcomer to get into groups of three. The idea being not to rearrange groups, but to *birth* them. This is a principle that will serve your group—and your church—well in the future. If you're not sure if your visitor is going to stick around, put your newcomer with a foursome.

• For your background music, use something that allows listeners to hear distinct instruments. You might choose something that includes a solo or two. The style of music isn't as important—or whether group members can tell a bass guitar from a stand-up bass, a saxophone from a trumpet, or a cello from a violin—as long as they can clearly hear different musicians playing their parts.

Even if you decide to do the movie option instead of the music discussion, the background music will still reinforce your lesson and create a better learning environment as well.

Session 3

- For the blindfold activity, make sure there's enough room for groups to move around and enough obstacles so people won't have an easy time when they're blindfolded. Don't make it *too* difficult, but have enough tables and chairs strewn about that groups will have to do a little bit of work.

  You might even make the suggestion that groups *could* lead their blindfolded people to the wrong seats—and thus mess up other groups' plans, too. It certainly would reinforce the message of this session that we're all connected—even when we don't think we are (or want to be).

- Are you praying for your group members regularly? It's the most important thing you can do for your group. Take time to pray right now, if you haven't already.

Session 4

- Now that you're a month into this season, you may find it helpful to make some notes right after the session to help you evaluate how things are going. Ask yourself, Did everyone participate? and Is there anyone I need to make a special effort to follow up with before the next session?

- This would also be a good opportunity to remind you that if you need to spend more than just one week on a given lesson—and if you're not tied to a calendar and *can* spend some extra time—then do it! Taking the time to understand what God wants to tell your class, group, or accountability partner(s) is *way* more important than "covering the material."

- If you do the opening activity in Come and See instead of the video clip, you *will* need something big to write on.

The white board won't be for recording people's answers this time around. Here's what you'll need to do: Write, "I didn't say you were ugly" in big letters so everyone will see the words. Don't comment on it as people arrive.

Session 5

- Are you the group leader? If not, I *told* you to wait. Now get back to the regular part of the session where you belong. Close the door on your way out, please.

  Seriously, stop peeking. *Now.*

- OK, leaders, now that we're finally alone, you're going to need two things: a small slip of paper and a $5 bill. You can use a $10 or $20 if you're feeling generous and/or want to make a bigger impact, but a $5 bill should get it done. And yes, you *are* going to give your bill away.

  On your slip of paper, write, "If you want to see change, focus on what you'll gain instead of what you'll lose."

  Keep your bill hidden at first; you can hold the slip of paper in your hand, if you like. If group members say, "I don't have a dollar," offer to accept their change or another item they have that they won't need back. Give them every opportunity to accept your offer.

  Give your volunteer the paper, but hang on to your bill until after you've discussed the question beginning, "What's one small positive change…" After your group has discussed it, hand your volunteer your bill, and say something like, "Remember: If you want to see change, focus on what you'll gain instead of what you'll lose."

  Give your volunteer a round of applause for his or her bravery and good fortune, and then continue your discussion.

- By now, you might be thinking, "Boy, leading this group sure is *costing* me." But when you think about it, that's part of *any* leadership, isn't it? Therefore, to give you a little reward and to remind you that the benefits of leading change *do* outweigh the costs, here's a brief devotional just for *you*.

> *Read Philippians 3:7-14. Then think through the questions that follow, and share your answers with God. He already knows the answers, but maybe you need to say them aloud. So listen for God's answers after you open this part of your life to him. Take as long as you need to really listen for God's voice.*
>
> - *How has being a leader already cost you?*
> - *Which costs had you expected? Which ones did you not see coming or totally underestimate?*
> - *What have you received from God that you wouldn't have received had you not given up those things?*
>
> *When you're done sharing with God, take some more time to thank him for the blessings you've received, even through the crucible of leadership.*

If you'd like to share the above devotional with the group, use it in Go, either in place of or along with the discussion of Romans 12:1-2. If God's spoken to you through this, I'd strongly encourage you to share what God's shared with *you*. And may God bless you for your faithfulness to your group.

And since you're already here, and we've already talked about the money issue…

- Take a peek ahead at the notes for Session 6. If you need to, think about collecting money after this session to pay for your supplies for next week.

Session 6

- Remember the importance of starting and ending on time, and remind your group of it, too, if you need to.
- In preparation for your opening activity, use as many beach balls as your meeting area (and budget) allows. One will get the message across, but the more you use,

the stronger your message. You could even buy a beach ball for every group member. (*Told* you leadership can be costly.) During the prayer time, have people hold a beach ball to represent those relationships you're all struggling with right now. Then have people take their beach balls home as reminders of today's lesson. The size of the beach ball(s) isn't critical. Also, be sure to safety-proof before your session. Put away anything fragile, and put any room lamps on the floor (or elsewhere) until the activity is done.

- Here's how you'll start: Get everyone seated. When you're ready (whether the *rest* of the group is or not), start randomly tossing your beach ball(s) around. Don't tell people how to react; just throw them out there and see what happens. Take a minute or so to have fun with this, and then start the discussion.

- By the way: You don't *have* to pay for everything. Another part of being a leader is knowing when it's time to share the responsibility (and there'll be sessions about *that* later on, too). If you like, or need to, ask for contributions from the group or church leadership to help defray personal costs. Do what it takes so your experiences are both doable and meaningful.

- One more thing: During your discussion of Acts 14–15, don't be shocked if the last question starts a debate within your group. Group members might even have opposing hot-button issues. Stay the course. Be respectful, and make sure the discussion stays that way, too. It could become a "live" discussion that sets up the next part of your session perfectly, as your smaller groups explore how *they* should approach differences with one another. In fact, you might want to put this book down and read 2 Timothy 2:23-26 right now, to prepare yourself.

- Also, this lesson isn't intended to cover disputes that have gotten to the point where pastoral intervention or even church discipline is needed, although some group members might be facing such a situation right now. Different churches handle disputes in different ways. If someone in your group is facing such a situation, make time to discuss it after your meeting time, and refer him or her to your church's leadership as needed.

- This would also be a good time to remind group members of the importance of following through on the weekly challenge each of them has committed to in Walk It Out.

Session 7

- Congratulations! You're halfway through this study. It's time for a checkup: How's the group going? What's worked well so far? What might you consider changing as you approach the remaining sessions?

- That's right: For the first 10 minutes of your session, just hang out as a group. Serve some snacks, and just let people talk. If your group's normally pretty social, stretch your "catch-up time" to include an extra 10 minutes. Also, feel free to play some background music, if that's what you normally do when you have company. Of course, play it at a level that allows people to talk (no blasting your favorite Christian "death metal" album!).

- For your closing prayer time, I strongly suggest sharing in the Lord's Supper together. It's always a significant experience to have with your group.

  That said, some groups won't be comfortable doing this, and some churches might even frown on the idea of sharing the Lord's Supper in a context other than your corporate worship service. If it's just a comfort factor, I'd ask you to push through it—it'll be worth it.

  Nonetheless, here's an alternative approach: Simply pass a loaf of bread around your group, letting everyone tear off a piece as it's passed around. Your group members will still understand the symbolism, and the significance, of what you're doing.

Session 8

- Read the food experience in Go beforehand to understand how your snack will be used, and prepare accordingly. I would have suggested pizza, but given its relatively short preparation time, and the long wait time during the session, it might be an interruption to your group and/or too cold for anyone to enjoy. (If not, go for it!) Pie or casserole will stay warmer longer. If your meeting area has an oven, you could even put your food in the oven beforehand and pull it out just before your experience.

  Either way, just the smells will enhance your group's experience and sense of anticipation. Of course, the taste will help, too!

Session 9

- How are you doing with your prayer time for the group? Take some time to pray for your group now, if you haven't done so already.

Session 10

- Now would be a good time to do another group checkup—especially if you're planning to do another study together after this. Ask yourself (and the group, if it makes sense to do so—but phrase it differently if you do), "Is everyone participating?" and "Is there anyone I need to make a special effort to follow up with?"

Session 11

- If possible, have three groups working together during the activity in Come and See, so there's a group lining up on each side and a third group trying to get through the line unscathed. If you have eight or fewer people, have everyone but the person walking with his or her candle become part of the corridor. Let people come out of the line one at a time to take the candle through the corridor so there'll still be enough people left in line.

• Follow up with your group members—or at least a representative from each smaller group—to make sure everyone's working through the spiritual health plan worksheets for Session 12. Encourage everyone to take the time to process what God wants to—and needs to—do in their lives next.

Session 12

• Since your next lesson will be your group's last one in this book, you'll probably want to start discussing with the group what to do after you've completed this study. Will you go on to Season Six? "Pull over" and study another subject in more depth? Will you break up and head to different classes? Make your plans now.

• Did you follow up with your group members before this session? If not, get to it! Make sure they're working through "My Spiritual Health Plan." You'll all be able to hit the ground running this week if you do.

• Also, take the time now to read the Leader Notes for Session 13. Take time before or after your session to recruit people to plan and bring food to the party you'll have next week. Even if they don't bring food, tell them to bring appetites. Or put down this book and start calling and planning right now!

Session 13

• Since this is your group's last session in this book, make sure you have a plan for next week…and beyond.

• Your party is a big piece of your session today. (Again, be sure to tell everyone beforehand to bring their appetites.)

Plan three courses—as simple or extravagant, as you like—but have three specific courses. It could simply be three different types of snack, such as candies, then chips, then cookies. Or you could be more elaborate and share an actual three-course meal, with appetizers, main course and dessert; doing so would bring out the meaning of the lesson even more vividly. Either way, make it clear which course is which. You could even put signs in front of each course to make it clearer.

Keep your first course very simple, as the second course will start about 10 minutes later. From there, it's up to you. You may even want to add a fourth course for after your session. Keep your party going as long as you like!

Make sure your meeting area is festive as well. Put up balloons, streamers, banners, or whatever else works for your group. Just make sure everyone who shows up today—and anyone who walks or drives by, for that matter—knows there's a party going on!

No matter what you do—congratulations! You've made it through Season Five of Growing Out! We hope God's blessed your walk together these past few months, and that you'll continue to let him lead all of you forward together.